Supporting ICT in the early years

Supporting early learning

Series Editors: Vicky Hurst and Jenefer Joseph

The focus of this series is on improving the effectiveness of early education. Policy developments come and go, and difficult decisions are often forced on those with responsibility for young children's well-being. This series aims to help with these decisions by showing how developmental approaches to early education provide a sound and positive basis for learning.

Each book recognizes that children from birth to 6 years old have particular developmental needs. This applies just as much to the acquisition of subject knowledge skills, and understanding as to other educational goals such as social skills, attitudes and dispositions. The importance of providing a learning environment that is carefully planned to stimulate children's own active learning is also stressed.

Throughout the series, readers are encouraged to reflect on the education being offered to young children, through revisiting developmental principles and using them to analyse their observations of children. In this way, readers can evaluate ideas about the most effective ways of educating young children and develop strategies for approaching their practice in ways that offer every child a more appropriate education.

Published titles

Jonathan Doherty and Richard Bailey: *Supporting Physical Development and Physical Education in the Early Years*
Bernadette Duffy: *Supporting Creativity and Imagination in the Early Years*
Lesley Hendy and Lucy Toon: *Supporting Drama and Imaginative Play in the Early Years*
Vicky Hurst and Jenefer Joseph: *Supporting Early Learning – The Way Forward*
Linda Pound and Chris Harrison: *Supporting Music in the Early Years*
Linda Pound: *Supporting Mathematical Development in the Early Years*
Iram Siraj-Blatchford and Priscilla Clarke: *Supporting Identity, Diversity and Language in the Early Years*
John Siraj-Blatchford and Iain McLeod-Brudenell: *Supporting Science, Design and Technology in the Early Years*
Marian Whitehead: *Supporting Language and Literacy Development in the Early Years*

Forthcoming titles

Caroline Jones: *Supporting Inclusion in the Early Years* (Spring 2004)

Supporting ICT in the early years

John Siraj-Blatchford and
David Whitebread

Open University Press

Open University Press
McGraw-Hill Education
McGraw-Hill House
Shoppenhangers Road
Maidenhead
Berkshire
England
SL6 2QL

email: enquiries@openup.co.uk
world wide web: www.openup.co.uk

First published 2003

A catalogue record of this book is available from the British Library

ISBN 0 335 20942 4 (pb)   0 335 20943 2 (hb)

Library of Congress Cataloging-in-Publication Data
CIP data has been applied for

Typeset by RefineCatch Limited, Bungay, Suffolk
Printed in the UK by Bell & Bain Ltd, Glasgow

Contents

Series editors' preface

This book is one of a series which will be of interest to all those who are concerned with the care and education of children from birth to 6 years old – childminders, teachers and other professionals in schools, those who work in playgroups, private and community nurseries and similar institutions; governors, providers and managers. We also speak to parents and carers, whose involvement is probably the most influential of all for children's learning and development.

Our focus is on improving the effectiveness of early education. Policy developments come and go, and difficult decisions are often forced on all those with responsibility for young children's well-being. We aim to help with these decisions by showing how developmental approaches to young children's education not only accord with our fundamental educational principles, but provide a positive and sound basis for learning.

Each book recognizes and demonstrates that children from birth to 6 have particular developmental learning needs, and that all those providing care and education for them would be wise to approach their work developmentally. This applies just as much to the acquisition of subject knowledge, skills and understanding, as to other educational goals such as social skills, attitudes and dispositions. In this series, there are several volumes with a subject-based focus, and the main aim is to show how that can be introduced to young children within the framework of an integrated and developmentally appropriate curriculum, without losing its integrity as an area of knowledge in its own right. We also stress the importance of providing a learning environment which is carefully planned for children's own active learning.

The present volume helps educators to present Information and Communications Technology (ICT) to children as tools and 'toys' which can be used creatively. It offers down-to-earth help for parents and others in making sound choices of new technologies, so supporting young children to develop their own control over them, and gain authorship within them.

Access for all children is fundamental to the provision of educational opportunity. We are concerned to emphasize anti-discriminatory approaches throughout, as well as the importance of recognizing that meeting special educational needs must be an integral purpose of curriculum development and planning. We see the role of play in learning as a central one, and one which also relates to all-round emotional, social and physical development. Play, along with other forms of active learning, is normally a natural point of access to the curriculum for each child at his or her particular stage and level of understanding. It is therefore an essential force in making for equal opportunities in learning, intrinsic as it is to all areas of development. We believe that these two aspects, play and equal opportunities, are so important that we not only highlight them in each volume in this series, but include separate volumes on them as well.

Throughout this series, we encourage readers to reflect on the education being offered to young children, by revisiting the developmental principles which most practitioners hold, and using them to analyse their observations of the children. In this way, readers can evaluate ideas about the most effective ways of educating young children, and develop strategies for approaching their practice in ways which exemplify their fundamental educational beliefs, and offer every child a more appropriate education.

The authors of each book in the series subscribe to the following set of principles for a developmental curriculum:

Principles for a developmental curriculum

- Each child is an individual and should be respected and treated as such.
- The early years are a period of development in their own right, and education of young children should be seen as a specialism with its own valid criteria of appropriate practice.
- The role of the educator of young children is to engage actively with

what most concerns the child, and to support learning through these preoccupations.

- The educator has a responsibility to foster positive attitudes in children to both self and others, and to counter negative messages which children may have received.
- Each child's cultural and linguistic endowment is seen as the fundamental medium of learning.
- An anti-discriminatory approach is the basis of all respect-worthy education, and is essential as a criterion for a developmentally appropriate curriculum (DAC).
- All children should be offered equal opportunities to progress and develop, and should have equal access to good quality provision. The concepts of multi-culturalism and anti-racism are intrinsic to this whole educational approach.
- Partnership with parents should be given priority as the most effective means of ensuring coherence and continuity in children's experiences, and in the curriculum offered to them.
- A democratic perspective permeates education of good quality, and is the basis of transactions between people.

Vicky Hurst and Jenefer Joseph

An integrated approach to ICT education

In supporting children in their development of an early understanding of Information and Communications Technology (ICT) we are concerned to support them in learning about a wide range of products that are used to manipulate, store, retrieve, transmit or receive information. Most of the ICT applications that we are familiar with today are put to use in electronic products such as telephones, audio and video, CD and cassette players/recorders, computers, and television receivers.

Throughout the book we will argue that the ICT guidance that is offered to early years practitioners within the UK in the *Curriculum Guidance for the Foundation Stage* (QCA/DfEE 2000) provides a sound basis for an appropriate curriculum in early childhood. But this is a curriculum that may be considered to consist of three quite separate and distinct strands, and we have found that early years practitioners and parents lack confidence and seek guidance in providing appropriate provision in all three areas. The first area is related to developing an emergent 'technological literacy', the second to developing information skills and capability in terms of 'communication', and the third to 'control'.

Communication and control will emerge as major themes throughout the book, but in this introductory chapter we argue the case for supporting children in their early development of technological literacy and explain more fully precisely what we mean by the term.

'Technological literacy' is a new form of literacy, but it is one that is increasingly considered to represent an essential curriculum entitlement in any broad and balanced curriculum for the twenty-first century. In fact, given the major effect that the new technologies are having on our lives and lifestyles, it is sometimes argued that technology should now be accepted as standing alongside literature, science and music in providing a major cultural form of representation in its own right (Sherman and Craig 1995; Kaput 1996; Fanning 2001). ICT products are increasingly supporting, regulating, facilitating, and *limiting* the things that people do, and the lives that they lead. ICT regulates how people gain access to information, and how they express themselves with it. ICT applications dominate the leisure activities of millions of people; they are also applied to determine how people communicate and transport themselves and how resources and food are distributed. Technicians and engineers are employed to create, maintain and operate these technologies and countless others to promote and market them. ICT has become an integral part of the political and economic system (Ellul 1980).

The provision of education for technological literacy may therefore be seen as a citizenship issue. For citizens (of any age) to make informed technological choices they must gain some understanding of the technologies that are available. To participate actively in the future development of their culture and economy they must be equipped to predict the impact and consequences of introducing new technologies on their social, biological and physical environment. In early education this begins with children learning about the new technology that is being applied around them, and becoming more aware of the critical technological choices that are being made by the adults that are significant to them. It also means being increasingly involved in making these choices themselves.

ICT encompasses a wide range of technological products and applications but the most significant for many of us in recent years has been the computer. Parents are increasingly providing desktop computing experience for their children at home, and significant numbers have now found their way into pre-school classrooms. It is therefore appropriate that a good deal of this book is concerned with providing the most appropriate uses of this technology for young children. Computer education is now widely considered to be a priority for young children as it is considered to be the technology of the future, and to represent a technology that is already having a profound influence upon our lives. But all of this raises an important question that we must consider first: Just how aware are we of the computer technology that is being applied around us? Imagine a fairly routine scenario involving a father collecting his 4-year-old child from the nursery:

> Having offered their thanks and farewells to the nursery staff the
> couple walk hand in hand across the pavement towards the car. As

they do so, the father answers a call on his mobile telephone. It is the child's mother, and she is calling to remind him that she had finished the milk that morning, and that they would need to visit the supermarket if they were to have anything to eat that evening. The couple drive to the supermarket, and along the way the child expresses surprise and delight as a set of traffic lights changes to green just as they are coming towards them. They stop at the supermarket and purchase all of the groceries that they will need for the next few days. The child watches as the sales assistant passes each of the products through the checkout, and as her father pays for the supplies using his credit card. They drive home and as they enter the house the two split up; the child throws herself on the sofa and begins to flick through the TV channels to see what is on. The father goes to the kitchen to load most of the food that he has bought into the refrigerator. One of the frozen food products is placed in the microwave oven and it is set to defrost for their evening meal.

It is sometimes difficult to recognize all of the applications of computers around us as they are increasingly embedded within other technological products. ICT is increasingly an invisible yet also a ubiquitous technology, and it really is having a profound effect upon our lives. From the moment that they left the classroom this father and his child were interacting with a wide range of special purpose computers. Most may be considered to have very little visibly in common with the 'desktop computer' that they both may have experienced working and playing with. It may even be the case that many adults fail to recognize them as computers. But most of these computers incorporate the same components and run programs in very much the same way as any other forms of computer, and we need to recognize that they represent as legitimate a part of an ICT education as any standard office workstation.

When the father answered the phone he was operating a computer. In a typical cellphone micro-processors are employed to control all of the routine background communications that need to be made with the base station in order to make and keep the connection throughout the call. Micro-processors are used to perform high-speed signal-manipulation calculations and they also coordinate the operations of all of the customizable features on the phone such as the directory of numbers.

From the moment the car was started at least one computer (often more), or 'microcontroller', was activated. As they drove along, this micro-controller will have been controlling the mixture of the fuel provided to the engine. Another microcontroller may have been controlling the anti-lock brakes. In many cars a microcontroller is employed to operate the cruise control facility and/or to provide information on fuel consumption and the number of miles that may be driven given the current level of fuel in the petrol tank.

As they approached the traffic lights the car passed over wires embedded in the road called 'loop detectors' which produced a signal that was transmitted to the local traffic computer. The traffic speed and the number of vehicles at the junction was determined by detecting how quickly the cars passed across two sets of these detectors. It was the central traffic computer that operated the traffic lights early to maintain the most efficient traffic flow through the junction.

At the supermarket, the combination of black bars and the spaces of varying widths between them on the bar code attached to each of the products that they purchased provided an encoded reference number that the supermarket computer used to access a more detailed record of the products' price, their current stock levels and other descriptive data. The information from the bar code was scanned into the computer at the checkout using a laser, and the computer instantly located the item in its database, and displayed the price on the cash register. These computerized checkout systems provide supermarkets with continuous information on the amount of money taken at each checkout, as well as the products that are sold. They also continuously monitor the store's inventory and identify the items that should be ordered to replenish the shelves.

When the sales assistant 'swiped' the father's credit card through the device on the counter, his customer details that had been recorded on the magnetic strip of the card were read off and transmitted directly to a local bank. The bank's computer then communicated electronically through the credit card network and passed on an authorization for the transaction. At the same time the debit was recorded against his account, and this would be communicated to him later in his monthly statement and bill.

Almost everything with a remote control incorporates a microcontroller. So even if it hadn't been the TV that the child switched on as she arrived home, she might have been interacting with a computer in a stereo system or some other device. Similarly, when the keypad of the microwave oven was pressed, a microcontroller operated the oven and provided the light emitting diode or liquid crystal display that confirmed the program that was being operated.

In fact, a wide range of other products incorporate computers that are dedicated to particular functions, and these microcontrollers are included in modern cameras, camcorders, answering machines, laser printers, telephones (those with caller ID, number memories, etc.), as well as any refrigerators, dishwashers, ovens, washers or dryers that have displays and keypads. This is to say nothing about the multitude of uses in industry, in commerce and in banking. We are also certain to see more and more of these devices incorporated in the technology around us as new applications are found for them. Cars are already being equipped with satellite navigation systems, and a US company has now produced a sophisticated optical lane departure warning system which warns sleepy drivers when they unintentionally begin to cross over into an adjacent traffic lane. Ford planned to begin installing this new technology in a range of their cars from 2003.

What is a Computer?

The mainframe computers used in industry, the desktop computers used in offices and at home, and the microcontrollers that are used in a wide variety of modern products all have several things in common. They all have a 'central processing unit' (CPU) that runs a 'program', they all have some form of 'memory' storage facility to hold that program, and they all have input and output devices that allow them to interact with the people or machinery the computer has been designed to serve. For a desktop computer the keyboard and mouse provide the main input devices and the monitor and printer the outputs. In the case of a television microcontroller the input comes from our operation of the remote control switches and the output appears on the TV screen.

What is a program?

Programs are used to control things, and electrical devices often need to be switched on and off in sequence to achieve a desired purpose. The domestic washing machine provides a very good example of this. Most washing machines are still controlled by a mechanical (rather than electronic) 'central processor' so that they also provide an excellent illustration of the principles employed in the very first computers manufactured by Charles Babbage in the nineteenth century. While the switching in a washing machine is usually carried out as an electric (or clockwork-driven) barrel rotates, the barrels in Babbage's 'Difference Engine' were cranked manually by turning a handle, but otherwise they functioned in a similar way:

> The barrels had studs fixed to their outer surface in much the same way as the pins of a music box or a barrel organ. The barrels orchestrated the internal motions of the engine. As the barrel turned, the studs activated specific motions of the mechanism and the position and arrangement of the studs determined the action and the relative timing of each motion.
>
> (Swade 2000: 97).

> On loading your clothes into a washing machine, you are usually required to select a 'program' that is determined by your decisions regarding the size of the load, the appropriate temperature of the water for the wash and rinse cycles, the length of these cycles, and the speed of agitation, and of the final spin. These decisions will in part depend upon the strength and nature of the fabrics that are to be washed (e.g. if they are delicate, woollen, dyed, heavy etc.), and on how soiled your clothes are. The choices that the operator has to make are often simplified according to the most common loads likely to be considered. After you fill the tub with clothes and switch on the program it is executed; a valve first opens to allow the machine to fill with water and then a heating element is switched on. As soon as the machine senses that it is full the valve is closed, and when it reaches the appropriate temperature the heating element is switched off as well. Then the clothes are stirred (or rolled) around by the agitator. After an appropriate period (and quality) of agitating, the drain valve is then opened and the water pumped out, and the machine then spins the clothes to remove most of the water. It refills, and agitates the clothes again to rinse out the soap. Then it drains and it spins again.

While computers were still considered something of a novelty just twenty years ago, we all now take for granted the technological improvements provided by desktop computers and the use of microcontrollers. The use of ICT in the early years has the potential to enhance educational opportunities for young children. It can be applied in a developmentally appropriate manner to encourage purposeful and exploratory play. It can encourage discussion, creativity, problem solving, risk taking and flexible thinking, and this can all be achieved in a play-centred and responsive environment. However, all of this does demand that practitioners are well trained and skilled in the appropriate uses of ICT with young children. ICT can also be misapplied in the early years and parents and professional educationalists and carers should therefore seek guidance to develop their skills in applying the most appropriate products, literature and research.

The Developmentally Appropriate Technology in Early Childhood (DATEC) project

Given the number and variety of educational computer programs (software) available on the market today there has been a growing need to provide early educators with guidance that assists them in identifying the most appropriate applications of ICT. In the USA the National Association for the Education of Young Children (NAEYC) published a position statement in April 1996 (updated February 1998) (Appendix A). More recently DATEC has published exemplars of good practice and guidance material for parents and early childhood educators to provide for the same purpose in the European context. DATEC was an initiative funded by the European Union in 1999–2001 and it is now sponsored by the IBM Corporation. The web-based resources were produced in research trials carried out in partnership with practitioners and researchers in Sweden, Portugal and the UK and they can now be found on http://www-datec.educ.cam.ac.uk.

In fact the DATEC initiative has contributed towards developing a growing consensus regarding the most appropriate forms that ICT education should take in early childhood (Siraj-Blatchford and Siraj-Blatchford 2003). In common with the UK Curriculum Guidance for the Foundation Stage (CGFS) and the National Curriculum (QCA/DfEE 2000), the DATEC partners agreed that the ICT curriculum should have two separate strands:

- the first related to developing an 'emergent technological literacy' and children's understanding of the uses of ICT;
- the second related to developing children's practical capability with the tools that ICT offers.

The DATEC approach presents ICT education within the broader framework of an integrated technology curriculum. ICT artefacts (hardware and software applications) are seen as 'tools' that are designed and made to serve particular purposes, and it is primarily in terms of these purposes that they should be open to initial evaluation. Just like any other technological artefacts, the tools of ICT carry values. They have been designed to serve particular social needs and they have particular uses. These must be identified in determining their educational value.

The DATEC guidance identifies eight general principles for determining the appropriateness of the ICT applications to be applied in the early years. We hope that these will not be interpreted in a simplistic way, but that parents and practitioners will use these points to engage in a discussion about each area and how it might fit into the general philosophy and practice of the particular setting. The guidance might also inform the ICT policy of early years settings or be used as a tool to evaluate software programs or other ICT applications.

1 Applications should be educational

An 'application' is defined by DATEC in simple terms of a 'use' of ICT. We might consider the application of a pretend mobile telephone in socio-dramatic play, or a computer program such as Build a Bug (from *Millie's*

Math House, Edmark) (Figure 1.1), integrated as a part of a more general project. The DATEC guidance suggests that the applications employed in the early years should be educational in nature and this effectively excludes all those applications where clear learning aims cannot be identified. However entertaining, most arcade-type games provide little encouragement of creativity, or indeed any other worthwhile learning outcome. This is not to suggest that applications should not be fun or enjoyable or used for leisure, only that they should be carefully chosen to have some educational potential as well. One of the most important implications of the emphasis that is placed here on 'applications' is that ICT products that were not originally intended for educational purposes may sometimes be effectively applied educationally by creative early childhood practitioners.

Many settings use language and number drill and practice programs explicitly for educational purposes, but DATEC found that many of these have very narrow educational aims (e.g. practising addition or learning colours). We therefore suggest that these be used with caution as they promote a very directive form of teaching, normally with the use of an external reward (a smiling face, a tick or a funny sound) and over-reliance on these kinds of program might lead to a reduction in children's intrinsic motivation to learn. So it isn't enough for applications to be educational, they must be developmentally appropriate as well. Children need a variety of applications that encourage a range of development including

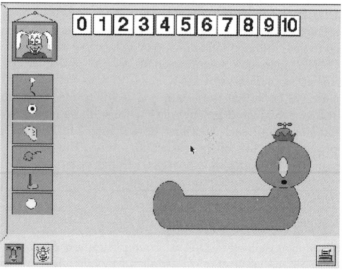

Figure 1.1 Build a Bug

creativity, self-expression and language. Applications should be employed after a thorough discussion with staff (and parents where this is possible) about the educational benefits and constraints of the particular application.

2 Encouraging collaboration

The best applications provide a valuable means of encouraging collaboration and in the early years we know that activities that provide contexts for collaboration are especially important. Working alone as well as in collaboration and in a range of other ways in interacting with technology is important too. However, according to Light and Butterworth (1992), 'joint attention' and 'children learning to share' and/or 'engaged jointly' provides a better cognitive challenge for young children. Siraj-Blatchford *et al.* (2001) have now provided even more evidence in support of what they term 'sustained shared thinking'. When children are engaged in pretend play together (socio-dramatic) this provides a context for children to share representations and to articulate their thinking, bringing to consciousness ideas that they are still only beginning to grasp intuitively (Hoyles 1985). Many screen-based applications offer the same possibilities in terms of symbolic manipulation although adult intervention is usually needed to gain the most from software that is designed to facilitate collaborative problem solving, drawing, or construction. Collaboration is also considered important in providing opportunities for cognitive conflict as efforts are made to reach consensus (Doise and Mugny 1984), and for the co-construction of potential solutions in the creative processes of problem solving (Forman 1989).

3 Integration and play through ICT

ICT applications should be integrated as far as possible with other established early years practices (play, project work) which make the curriculum relevant to the children. The adequacy of much of the ICT educational provision currently provided in schools is open to question in this regard. Primary schools are increasingly opting for computer suites, and this often discourages the integration of ICT with the rest of the curriculum. If children are to understand ICT they need to see it used in a meaningful context, and for real purposes. The DATEC exemplars show excellent examples where children have used, for example, a draw program to make part of a birthday card and then completed it using other materials and resources. Another example is where adults have taken children with them to a pre-school laundry room and explained and discussed the program cycles for hot and cold washes. This gives children an understanding of the purposes and uses of ICT as a tool to solve real problems.

Play is usefully considered a 'leading activity' for young children; and it is widely considered to be a driving force in the child's development of new forms of motivation and action. Play and imitation are primary contexts for representational and symbolic behaviour, and role-play is therefore central to the processes of learning in the early years. Artefacts such as toys and other 'manipulables' are important because they provide symbols for the children to play with. When children play with both functioning and pretend technological artefacts such as telephones or photocopiers they serve the same purpose. Computer applications also provide a means by which children may engage and interact with a much wider range of 'virtual' artefacts and environments than would otherwise be possible.

This is clearly recognized in the context of emergent literacy and numeracy where educators specifically encourage the child to recognize the value of using symbols to represent artefacts and to quantify them. But a great deal can be done to promote these processes in the wider play context and in children's play with technological toys.

Another very important reason for employing an integrated approach to ICT is the recognition that this is more consistent with the notion of ICT products as tools. Tools are designed to be applied for particular purposes when required; they are not usually designed for continuous use for their own sake. The common practice of operating a rota for children to gain access to computers may be seen as entirely contrary to this approach. Equally inappropriate is the common practice of providing access to ICT as a reward (or a punishment).

4 The child should be in control

Generally, applications should be controlled by the child; they should not control the child's interaction through programmed learning or any other behaviourist device. While the evidence suggests that applications of this kind may be effective in developing a range of skills including children's alphabet and phonic skills, counting and early number concepts, the approach is contrary to popular conceptions of good educational practice. There is a real consensus among informed early childhood educators across Europe regarding the importance of developing children's emergent awareness and positive disposition towards literacy and numeracy, and it may very well be the case that programmed learning approaches can operate against these principles. A similar case can be made against applications that incorporate 'closed' problem solving; problems that have only one solution. One of the best strategies for solving this sort of problem is simply to try every possible option until you find the right one and this is also the strategy that most children adopt. The irony is that this is precisely the strategy that computers are usually designed to adopt, and given the speed at which they can test the outcomes it is a strategy that they excel in. The kinds of problems that computers struggle with are the sort that have multiple solutions and where the real intellectual challenge is to clarify the problem sufficiently well to recognize when the best solution has been found. Arguably it is just this sort of creative problem solving we should be giving children practice in.

5 Applications should be transparent and intuitive

As far as possible, applications should be selected that provide 'transparency'; their functions should be clearly defined and intuitive. What this normally means in practice is that the application completes each clearly defined task in a single operation. The intuitive nature of the 'drag and drop' facility on a computer screen is a good example. Another good example of this functional transparency is provided by the Sony Mavica digital camera that saves images onto a floppy disk. When a photograph is taken, the disk is removed (with the photo on it) and when it is put into the computer, a double-click brings the picture directly onto the screen.

6 Applications should not contain violence or stereotyping

Unfortunately we cannot assume that all of the software finding its way into early years contexts is 'tasteful and dignified', but all applications should satisfy (for example) the Advertising Standards Authority code of practice (see Chapter 6). What we are suggesting here is that where applications fail to meet these criteria it would be difficult to justify their use in any educational context.

7 Awareness of health and safety issues

Serious concerns have been voiced about the consequences of encouraging the extended use of desktop computers by young children (Healey 1998). DATEC has reviewed the evidence on this matter and argues that the time spent using any desktop computer application by a child should be comparatively short, normally not extending beyond 10–20 minutes at a time in the case of 3-year-olds. DATEC suggests that this might be extended to a maximum of 40 minutes by the age of 8. Clearly, if a child or group of children is totally engaged in an activity and the completion of this requires a longer period at the computer this should be allowed, but it is argued that it would not be desirable to encourage children to do this regularly. Apart from the very significant difficulties of providing ergonomic, yet communal, workstations, these concerns relate to the hazards of repetitive strain injury, carpal tunnel damage, effects upon sight, the encouragement of sedentary behaviour and obesity, and the possible risks of radiation exposure from monitors. All of these hazards are well documented in the case of usage by adults but little research has been conducted to identify the implications for the youngest children at this early stage of their physical development.

The evidence regarding the degree of risk associated with these hazards remains unclear; but the precedent set by the UK government in discouraging children's use of mobile telephones in schools is instructive. The hazards of that technology were equally unclear yet the government's decision suggested that where we consider the safety of children, the burden of proof should lie on those introducing a new technology into schools rather than those who would urge caution. By limiting the time children spend at computers we can help to avoid some of these dangers for children. Where the computer use is integrated with other activities (and the computer used effectively as a tool), for instance in socio-dramatic play, modelling, painting etc., children will benefit from greater movement and exercise away from the computer. See Appendix B.

8 The educational involvement of parents

Research also suggests that *home–school communication* leads to better understanding and more positive attitudes by teachers and parents about each other's roles. Many studies have shown that when parents, teachers and children collaborate towards the same goals it leads to the improved academic performance of children (Siraj-Blatchford *et al.* 2001). Schools also report that children show a more positive attitude towards learning and are better behaved. Home–school links or parent involvement are therefore components of effective schools that merit special consideration. When home–school communication is well planned it can promote higher success in pupils and lead to more successful family environments. But many staff are ill equipped to know what kinds of strategies to adopt to foster better home–school relationships. In the United States the large-scale and longitudinal studies have been conducted by Epstein

(1996). Applying Epstein's typology, five main types of home–school improvement can be identified:

1 parenting skills, child development, and home environment for learning;
2 communications from school to home;
3 parents as volunteers in school;
4 involvement in learning activities at home;
5 decision making, leadership, and governance.

While a great deal is often achieved in terms of 1–3, most early childhood educational settings find 4–5 particularly challenging (Siraj-Blatchford *et al.* 2001). Communication between professional educators and parents is crucial in the early years and a more articulated set of aims between the home and early years setting can lead to better outcomes for children. Research carried out in the IBM KidSmart evaluation (Siraj-Blatchford and Siraj-Blatchford 2002a) shows that currently there is very little knowledge in pre-school settings about the children's ICT experiences at home and that this not an area on which parents are normally asked for information.

The CGFS *and 'emergent technology'*

As the UK 'Early Learning Goals' in the Curriculum Guidance for the Foundation Stage (CGFS) (QCA/DfEE 2000) now suggest, before children complete their fifth year they should be finding out about and identifying the uses of technology in their everyday lives, and they should also be using computers and programmed toys to support their learning. The CGFS also usefully suggests that we should encourage children to observe and talk about the uses of ICT in the environment, for example on local walks adults can talk with children about traffic lights, telephones, street lights or bar code scanners which identify product prices in shops. The Early Learning Goals and CGFS are set within a play-centred and child-centred philosophy of early education where appropriate pedagogies of modelling, demonstration, positive adult–child interaction, and responsive relations are paramount, and we promote this philosophy throughout the following pages. In common with the CGFS, we will present the ICT curriculum throughout this text as an 'emergent' curriculum (Siraj-Blatchford and Siraj-Blatchford 2002b; Siraj-Blatchford, 2003).

An 'emergent technology curriculum' may be considered similar to any other 'emergent' curriculum. Just as the teachers who teach emergent literacy encourage 'mark making' as a natural prelude to writing, in emergent technology we encourage the child's playful 'application' of technology. Teachers who teach emergent literacy *read* a range of different kinds of text to children and in the same way, as emergent technology teachers, we should introduce the children to 'new applications'. We should provide them with the essential early experiences that they must have if they are to go on to understand and be empowered by technology in their later lives. These early experiences will include playing with a range of different technological artefacts and software products (real and pretend telephones, cameras, computers and so on). They will also include drawing children's attention to the uses of technology in the world around them. We can encourage 'technology play' in the nursery, setting up pretend office play environments, supermarket checkouts, and bank cash points for children to integrate into their play. Just as teachers who teach emergent literacy provide positive role models by showing children the value they place in their own use of print, in 'emergent technology' we can do the same by demonstrating and talking about our own use of technology. In so doing we will be encouraging the children to develop an emergent awareness of the nature and value of these resources for themselves. They will also be developing positive dispositions towards the kind of technological applications that will be experienced in the future. It will be these positive attitudes and beliefs about the importance of the subject that, more than anything else, influence their motivation to engage in the subject in the future.

Another thing that many educators committed to emergent literacy do is to encourage parents to read to their children and ensure that the children see them reading for their own purposes. Large-scale research projects looking at the development of early literacy have shown the enormous value of parents reading to children and taking them to the library (Melhuish *et al.* 2001). In a similar way pre-schools may develop parental partnerships that contribute towards coordinated efforts in developing technological literacy.

2

ICT *in the home, the local environment and early years education*

Is ICT *good for young children?*

In many ways, this is a very difficult time to be writing about young children's use of new technologies and their possible educational applications. This is partly because the technologies themselves are in a period of unprecedented change which still seems to be accelerating. Whether young children's capabilities in all kinds of areas are limited by developmental constraints, or by the current limitations of the technology available to them, is still very much an open question. How well will they be able to use a device strapped to their wrists which combines the functions of a digital camera and camcorder, a mobile phone, a WebCam, and a fully voice-sensitive computer with email and internet access? We simply don't know, but within the next few years, we are surely going to find out.

At the same time, there is continuing controversy about the degree to which it is appropriate or 'healthy', in any case, for parents or early years educators to encourage young children to engage with ICT and related new technologies. Just two recent examples from the media illustrate some of the important features of this debate. At one extreme, there is Jane Healy, an American educational psychologist whose views were reported in the *Observer* (16 April 2001) under the headline 'Computers rot our children's brains'. She told the Parent Child 2000 conference that providing pre-school children with access to computers was: 'damaging the brain development in the sense that it's going to make it harder for them to learn at school'. Taking a very different view, however, other researchers have argued that even apparently violent computer games, which understandably cause concern among many parents and teachers, can be beneficial to children's learning. Under the headline 'Violent games spark creativity' (*Times Educational Supplement*, 28 September 2001), research was reported into the game playing of 11-year-old boys carried out by Julia Gillen and Nigel Hall of Manchester Metropolitan University. They found evidence that some apparently violent games nevertheless incorporated significant opportunities for creativity. These games: 'involved problem-solving skills, encouraged the children to use different resources such as the internet and fostered a willingness to persist in a task in the face of obstacles'.

This chapter attempts to address some of the questions raised by these kinds of positions. It argues that the benefits to young children and their learning of well-chosen ICT experiences far outweigh any potential dangers. We should also keep an open mind as to young children's capabilities in this area. There are, however, a range of concerns about current practice both in the home and in educational settings. The chapter concludes by suggesting ways forward in terms of developing stronger links and continuities between the child's experiences of new technologies and their use in the home, their community and the school.

Let us first address the issue of the appropriateness of ICT experience for young children. Some early years educators take a simple ideological stand on this. Followers of Steiner Waldorf education, for example, take the position that children should play only with 'natural, non-manufactured materials', and so not only exclude the full range of new information and communication technologies, but also any item made of plastic – Lego, for example. There is much to admire in Steiner education, and, on balance, our view would be that it is to the credit of the DfES that Steiner schools have recently been exempted from the requirement to teach ICT in order to qualify as providers of Foundation Stage education. The Steiner position on technology is illogical (some manufactured items such as woollen cloths are happily incorporated) and, like all belief systems, is the product of the historical and cultural circumstances in which it originated. The objection to 'manufactured' and 'mechanical' artefacts is more a reaction against the dehumanizing aspects of nineteenth-century industrialization than it is a reasoned assessment of twenty-first century children's needs. However, what is hugely valuable in the Steiner position, of course, is the emphasis on simplicity of resources and on encouraging children's use of their imagination. We would argue, however, that this position is not incompatible with the use of ICT; indeed, as we have already suggested in the first chapter, and as we shall attempt to demonstrate repeatedly later in the book, ICT applications themselves vary markedly in the opportunities they offer for imagination and creativity, and this is a vital test of their value. Our position, then, is that an evaluation of the educational value of new technologies should not be based on what they are made of, but on what opportunities they offer for children in terms of activities and experiences.

Other early years educators opposed to offering ICT opportunities within educational settings for young children take the less extreme view that such opportunities are fine, but that there are other, more sensory-based experiences and practical activities that young children will benefit from more. This is also, of course, a very well-founded position. Young children are physically active and do learn most effectively in multi-sensory ways. Another important aspect of early years education, however, has always been to introduce children to culturally important symbolic forms of representation (language, drawing, art, stories, drama, dance, modelling etc.) and the associated cultural and physical tools. The new information and communication technologies are intimately bound up in these aspects of human activity. Indeed, as many commentators have noted (see, for example, Sefton-Green 1999), one of the more exciting aspects of the emergence of the new technologies is the plethora of tools they are providing for children and adults alike to construct new forms of representation and of artistic and creative expression. As Sefton-Green argues, it is not only that we now have computer games, hyper-linked websites, digital image manipulation software, 'sampling' of MIDI music files and so on, but that 'the increasing accessibility of these technologies has created significant new opportunities for young people to become cultural producers, rather than mere consumers' (Sefton-Green 1999: 2).

This is clearly of very considerable significance for children's learning. Indeed, it is increasingly being argued by psychologists and neuro-scientists that the current ICT revolution may well have a significance in terms of human development equivalent to those which occurred when language itself first evolved and during the emergence of literacy. Evidence from studies of the evolution of the brain (e.g. Wills 1994; Deacon 1997) has suggested that the early emergence of the ability for symbolic representation in the form of language was pivotal in the development of the human brain. The impact of literacy on aspects of children's intellectual development has also been clearly established (Olson *et al.* 1985; Francis 1987). These kinds of fundamental changes in the ways in which our brains receive and represent information, it is argued, are also very much a part of the current ICT developments. For example, the increasing use of visual forms and the consequent demands on visual literacy are well documented. The non-linear forms of information presentation made possible by hypertexts is another example. (Note: the term 'hypertext' is applied to describe the use of 'hot buttons' that provide active links between different pages of textual or visual information.)

Evidence of the quite rapid improvements in general intelligence through recent generations (Flynn 1994), furthermore, has demonstrated the continuing capacity of the human brain to respond to increasing novelty and complexity in the environment. The explosion of the extent to which ICT technologies are rapidly becoming part of our everyday lives clearly adds to this kind of complexity of cognitive demand. All this, combined with the now clearly established significance of early educational experience for children's life chances (Sylva and Wiltshire 1993), compels us to take very seriously the notion that young children should be given the opportunity to experience new technologies in their early years of schooling. This is perhaps particularly the case in the situation to which we will refer in the next section of this chapter, in which young children have unequal access to ICT technologies within their home environments.

Our belief is that many of the objections of some early educators to the introduction of ICT into early years education are founded on the belief that it encourages children to be passive recipients, that it is isolating, and that young children cannot learn effectively from this kind of experience. On the contrary, as we want to argue in the later parts of this book, the use of appropriate ICT technology can be a very active, social, intellectually stimulating and liberating experience for young children, which opens up new possibilities for them in a variety of areas. In our experience, when early years educators have seen the joy and enthusiasm with which young children interact with a programmable toy, a working intercom or telephone link between classes, a digital camera and associated computer graphics package, an interactive whiteboard or a problem-based computer game, many of their objections disappear. As is often the case, the best judges of what is developmentally appropriate for young children are the children themselves, and they overwhelmingly respond with unreserved enthusiasm to the 'magical' possibilities of well-chosen new technologies.

The descriptor 'well-chosen' is, of course, crucial. As with any educational resource, the new technologies can be used well or badly. What evidence we have, furthermore, suggests that to date neither parents nor educators are making the best possible choices about the provision for their children in this area.

Children's use of ICT at home and school

As we have established in Chapter 1, young children today are growing up in a world which not only contains but is also increasingly shaped by ICT. A number of researchers concerned with the experiences of childhood, with the proliferation of ICT, with cultural changes, and with early education, have made studies of the impact of the new technologies on the lives of young children. In broad terms the conclusions that may be reached from these studies thus far are that

- new ICT technologies are impacting considerably on young children's lives;
- young children have very differential access to new ICT technologies;
- parents are sometimes unaware of their children's exposure to these technologies and the material that can be transmitted via them;
- parents vary in their ability to provide appropriate experiences and support for their children;
- many children have much greater access to new ICT technologies in the home than they do in educational settings;
- teachers are often under-informed and lacking confidence in relation to ICT;
- the provision of ICT in early years educational settings varies considerably, and is often very limited;
- communication between parents and educators about children's experiences in this area is often non-existent.

These conclusions do not, clearly, present a very happy picture of the experience of ICT by young children in either the home or the school environment at the present moment. Opportunities are being missed and both parents and teachers need to be better informed as to what these might be and what might be developmentally appropriate ICT experiences for young children.

The extent and nature of the impacts on children's lives of the new technologies has been most recently reviewed by Hutchby and Moran-Ellis (2001), who have brought together a very wide-ranging collection of papers originally presented at a conference on children, technology and culture at Brunel University in 1998. What emerges from a number of the pieces of research reported here, carried out in several different countries, is that the relations between children's lives and the new technologies are extensive and complex. Different cultural practices and domestic arrangements, together with different social norms among peer groups, impact upon children's experiences. Thus, the extent of non-organized, non-adult supervised time varies enormously between cultures (high in Finland, but low in Spain). Social norms among peer groups vary in the extent to which they are favourably or unfavourably disposed towards particular new technologies (some of which are 'cool', while others are only of interest to 'nerds' or 'geeks'). Some of these kinds of cultural and social norm variations, of course, are also markedly related to gender.

As a consequence of these kinds of cultural values and practices, but also as a consequence of socio-economic factors, young children's experiences of the new technologies are very varied. In many countries, for example, there has been a quantum leap in the last few years in terms of domestic computer and internet access. The 'digital divide' between the technology-rich and technology-poor, however, remains a reality for many low-income, indigenous and geographically isolated families even in such generally technologically advanced countries as Australia and the United States (Australian Bureau of Statistics 2001; US Department of Commerce 2000). An international study by the Intercultural Development Research Association (IDRA 2001) also found a range of cultural beliefs among a significant minority of children and adults who consequently had no experience with computers and no intention of buying or using one.

Within the UK a recent survey of technology use in the home was carried out by one of the present authors with a socially mixed sample of parents and their nursery-aged children (3–4 year olds) (Siraj-Blatchford and Siraj-Blatchford 2002a). From a list of technological devices including telephone, cassette recorder, washing machine, video recorder, electronic toy and computer, the results suggested that only the television was available in 100 per cent of homes. Where these various devices were available, however, with the exception of the washing machine, significant proportions of these young children used them, often unsupervised. There were also marked differences in use between different socioeconomic classes and between boys and girls. For example, 65 per cent of homes contained a computer, and 67 per cent of the boys, and 61 per cent of the girls, in these homes used them. Of the children who made use of the home computer, 47 per cent of boys did so without parental support, while this figure for girls was only 26 per cent. Of the homes containing computers, approximately two-thirds contained parents who were involved in 'middle-class' occupations and only one-third were involved in 'working class' occupations.

What is clear and universal, however, is that children have very different attitudes to new technologies from those of their parents. The anxieties of most parents about where new technologies are leading us are not shared by their children who, for obvious reasons, simply accept them as part of their everyday lives and proceed to explore their possibilities, often in highly creative and surprising ways. Some of this parental anxiety, of course, is concerned with the impact of technology, and some of the experiences it provides, on their children. Ironically, however, there is a good deal of evidence that many parents have little knowledge of their children's interaction with various ICT technologies. The study by Sanger *et al.* (1997) is typical of work in this area. This involved intensive interviewing and observation of around 100 children aged 4–9 years, together with their teachers and members of their families, in the years 1994–96. Sanger and his colleagues present a bleak picture of young children's interactions with screen-based video and computer-games materials, noting mostly parental apathy, teacher ignorance and child exploitation:

> Most children lead a rather unmediated experience within the theatre of the screen. They are not being educated and supported to develop a critical awareness of their experiences . . . in the face of powerful commercial forces. The ignorance of adults, regarding children's activities involving computers, computer games, the internet and videos means that issues involving, for example, gender, emotional impact, aggression, IT skills development, alienation, reading and writing, the interface between reality and fantasy and a whole host of other interrelated themes, documented in this research, are not being raised within educational settings.
>
> (Sanger *et al.* 1997: 169)

As we shall explore later in the book, we would wish to agree strongly with the view that technological literacy and critical awareness must be central to an educational ICT curriculum, but we clearly have work to do in this area within early years educational settings. In the words of Sanger *et al.*, as regards ICT education, helping children 'to develop control over the technology and authorship within it should be at the heart of education' (p. 172). At the moment, it simply is not. It is one of the primary aims of this book to help early years educators to begin to make sure that it is.

A significant part of the problem, Sanger found, was that many of the children's teachers rejected all domestically orientated computer games as being unworthy of their attention and of no possible relevance to the children's education. In fact, they found that many children played and enjoyed games such as 'Theme Park' and 'Sim City' (simulation games involving you in designing and building various kinds of complex environments), text- and image-based adventure games and problem-solving games like 'Tetris', and derived a good deal of clearly educative value from them. Their educational value, in terms of developing children's creative or logical thinking, was not, however, being as fully exploited as it might have been, either by parents mediating these experiences in the home, or by educators using them constructively as part of the children's formal educational experience. This finding was supported by researchers contributing to a major conference sponsored by the National Children's Bureau in 1995 (Gill 1996). Research reported by Mark Griffiths concluded that adult fears of the deleterious effects of game playing were largely unfounded. Only a small proportion of children (less than 10 per cent) were involved in heavy game use. While some of this game playing was, of course, of the violent combat type, many of the games favoured by the vast majority of children contained little or no violent imagery, and some apparent educational value (this issue of the educational potential of computer games is returned to in Chapter 5). However, there is some evidence that parents' abilities to buy ICT toys and games judiciously for their children is quite limited. Levin (2001) has reported early findings from an ongoing study of the use of ICT by children under 5 in their homes. She found a number of homes which contained vast collections of electronic toys which were largely being ignored by the children in favour of older, simpler and more traditional toys. The issue of simplicity and opportunities for young children to express their creativity and imagination arises very powerfully once more.

Both Sanger *et al.* (1997) and Gill (1996) also contain ample evidence of the domination of the domestic ICT scene by males (with the glaring exception of the washing machine, which we found in our survey is still only being used by 4.7 per cent of the male population!). The significance of this issue in relation to early years education, dominated as it is by female educators and role models, will be examined in the next chapter. Various commentators have surmised that this goes some way to explaining the relative paucity of provision in early years educational settings, and there is certainly ample evidence that young children's ICT experiences in school are lagging way behind those at home and in their community. A study by Mumtaz (2001), for example, of 360 primary aged children, found that children made far more use of computers at home than at school. Furthermore, the most common use in school was tasks related to word processing, which the children largely regarded as boring, while the most common use at home was game playing, to which the children were far more favourably disposed. A number of studies have also found that the level of children's use of computers in school is directly influenced by their experience of them out of school (e.g. Shoffner 1990), which raises obvious concerns about equity of access. Other studies (e.g. Giacquinta *et al.* 1993) have found considerable variation in the level of parental involvement and support for young children's ICT use, and that this was positively related to young children's ability and disposition to use computers for educational purposes. Issues of access and attitudes will be looked at in more depth in Chapter 3 when we consider significant aspects of individual children's ICT educational needs.

Of course, the situation is a rapidly changing one, both in the home and in educational settings, and we are clearly in an interim period. As today's game-playing, internet-accessing, website publishing teenagers become tomorrow's parents and early years educators, many of the present dislocations may disappear, or at least ameliorate. What is clear, however, is that the educational potential of the new technologies are not being at all well exploited at present. In order to move to a situation where they are, we need to concern ourselves principally with two areas. First, we need to re-examine the opportunities and experiences that ICT technologies offer in relation to young children's learning. Here we can learn something by looking at children's use of ICT in the home, and we need to look at ways of encouraging play with technology. Second, we need to explore ways in which parents and educators together can work to provide young children with a much more richly mediated experience of ICT, in part to help develop their critical awareness of it. These are the two issues to which the remainder of this chapter is addressed.

Play and 'emergent technology'

The Next Generation Forum (1999), an active American-based research group, have collected evidence from educational settings across the world about the educational uses of ICT technology with young children. They use this evidence to argue persuasively that the new technologies can be very powerful in supporting the creative potential of young children. Within this, they argue that young children learn overwhelmingly by playing with toys and tools, and so we must present ICT technology to children as technological toys and creative tools. If we can do this, they argue, these technological toys and tools can change important aspects of children and their learning:

- they change the learning relationships between children and teachers;
- the technology empowers children by granting them a voice they have never had before;
- they open novel ways of designing dynamic things which put children in touch with ideas and concepts that used to be beyond their reach;

- they foster change in learning strategies;
- they open new pathways to social interaction.

(Next Generation Forum 1999: 39)

Just three examples will give a flavour of the kind of approaches they have in mind. The first is the example of the children's conference in Costa Rica, where children from across the country bring designs and presentations to show to other children, usually based on a theme such as 'children's rights' or 'sustainable development'. The children use a range of technological tools to research and design their presentations, supported by their teachers. The second is the example of 'digital manipulatives' which are being developed at the Media Laboratory of The Massachusetts Institute of Technology (MIT) and trialled with young children. These include 'programmable bricks' (known as Lego Mindstorms in their commercial form); 'programmable beads' that can be used to make necklaces to emit light in different patterns; the 'bitball', a transparent, rubbery ball that can be programmed to light up in different colours depending on speed etc.; and 'thinking tags' which are based on traditional badges, but with built-in electronics so that they can communicate with one another (*Star Trek* fans have known about these for years!). The third example is research which showed that the 8th-grade students of teachers in the USA who used computers mainly for simulations and applications involving higher order thinking performed better on national tests than students in classes where the computers were used mainly for drill and practice.

This notion of technological toys and creative tools is clearly a very important one. The links between play and creativity have now been well established by research in child development and the psychology of human learning, and some reflection on the nature of these links makes it clear why this is a particularly relevant consideration in relation to the new technologies and the opportunities they offer.

Psychologists have been researching and developing theories about the nature and purposes of children's play since the middle of the nineteenth century. It has been suggested as a mechanism for letting off steam, for providing relaxation, for relieving boredom, for practising for adult life, for living out our fantasies and many more. That it is important in children's development, however, has never been in doubt. As Moyles (1989) demonstrated, for every aspect of human development and functioning, there is a form of play.

It is only in the last twenty to thirty years, however, that its significance for thinking, problem solving and creativity has been fully recognized. Bruner (1972), in a famous article entitled 'The nature and uses of immaturity', is generally credited with first pointing out to psychologists and educationalists the relationship across different animal species between the capacity for learning and the length of immaturity, or dependence upon adults. He also pointed out that as the period of immaturity lengthens, so does the extent to which the young are playful. He argued that play is one of the key experiences through which young animals learn, and also the means by which their intellectual abilities themselves are developed.

The human being, of course, has a much greater length of immaturity than any other animal, plays more and for longer, and is supreme, of course, in flexibility of thought. Play is significant in this, Bruner argues, because it provides opportunities to try out possibilities, to put different elements of a situation together in various ways, to look at problems from different viewpoints. This accords very closely to Anna Craft's (2000) recent definition of creativity as 'possibility thinking'. In this excellent book Craft demonstrates that creativity in this sense is not, as it is often conceived, a process confined to the arts, but a fundamental aspect of human learning, properly applicable across the curriculum. That the twenty-first century child needs to be a flexible thinker, who is able to be a creative mathematician, or scientist, or businessman, or engineer, or teacher, or administrator, or even politician, is clearly not in doubt.

Bruner demonstrated this relation between play, creativity and problem solving in a series of experiments (Sylva *et al.* 1976) in which children were asked to solve practical problems. Typically in these experiments, one group of children was given the opportunity to play with the objects involved, while the other group was 'taught' how to use the objects in ways which would help solve the problem. Consistently, the 'play' group subsequently outperformed the 'taught' group when they were left alone to tackle the problem. The children who had the experience of playing with the materials were more inventive in devising strategies to solve the problem, they persevered longer when their initial attempts did not work, and so were not surprisingly more successful in their attempts to solve the problem.

As a consequence of the freedom it offers to try things out, change things, etc., ICT offers particularly powerful opportunities to be playful in the way that Bruner has described. Only recently, one of the present authors was working with some 3-year-olds on a program which required them to enter their names. They were quite interested to see what their name looked like on the computer, and rather thrilled that you could change the size, and the font, and the colour, but they were overjoyed to discover that if you hold your finger down on a key the computer produces an endless stream of letters. And, if you then hold your finger down on the delete key they all disappear again! This discovery produced endless mirth and what seemed like hours of fun. Along the same lines is children's consistent delight, which we have observed repeatedly, in deliberately pressing the wrong button, or giving the wrong answer, to see what will happen. This playful approach is very much to be encouraged and enjoyed within the context of ICT technologies. Children who are allowed to play around with technology and explore different possibilities will be much more creative and effective in subsequently using it and solving problems with it.

Observation of children at play gives some indication of why it might be such a powerful learning medium. During play children are usually totally engrossed in what they are doing. It is quite often repetitive and contains a strong element of practice. During play children set their own level of challenge, and so what they are doing is always developmentally appropriate (to a degree which tasks set by adults will never be). Play is spontaneous and initiated by the children themselves; in other words, during play children are in control of their own learning. This is a theme that we will return to in Chapter 4.

The role of adults and developing home–school links

Of course, the most overwhelmingly significant element of young children's experience to affect the quality of their development, learning and self-identity is the quality of their early relationships with their parents and other significant adults (Schaffer 1977). The most powerful predictor of the ease and enthusiasm with which a young child becomes a reader, as we have also noted, is well known to be the degree of parental involvement in the child's early experiences of books, stories, rhymes and so on. As we have seen, this contrasts starkly with the present position as regards technological literacy. Early years settings are, however, particularly well placed to address this issue, as building strong home–school links has always been a high priority and there is considerable expertise among early years educators in this area. What is exciting, furthermore, about ICT technology is that it can itself be part of the answer.

As we have seen earlier in the chapter, children's experiences of ICT at home vary considerably. When they enter their early years setting or school environment they bring with them very different ICT experiences that are perhaps related to their gender and to their parents' own use of ICT. Children also may start to have stereotyped views about which equipment is appropriate for boys and girls to use. It is important, therefore, that as early years educators we attempt to involve parents in their young children's ICT education.

There is lots of encouragement in the *Curriculum Guidance for the Foundation Stage* (QCA/DfEE 2000) to build on children's experiences in the home and in their environment. Parents can very usefully be involved in a number of these activities. The 'stepping stones' set out within this curriculum framework suggest, for example, that children should be encouraged to become aware of technology around them in the early years educational setting, local environment and home, for example washing machines, traffic lights, telephones, street lights, cash registers, barcode scanners and burglar alarms. They should be given opportunities to operate simple equipment and taught simple skills of using equipment, for example switching on and off.

It seems important that schools provide parents with information as to what the children are capable of achieving with the ICT technology, including the computer, and provide some sort of training to parents. In helping to provide an educationally sound environment for the child Straker (1993), for example, concluded that there should be facilities for parents, governors and teachers to discuss the work that the children are doing with ICT and computers. If parents are to be involved in this process they should have guidelines. This is very important especially when parents have to decide when to intervene and when not. Straker (1993) proposed the following strategies to promote collaboration between parents, children and schools in young children's ICT education:

- Workshops for parents in small groups, where they could talk about children's work with ICT and at the computer.
- Arrangements where parents can observe children at work. For example, when a child's parents arrive, they and their child should have some time together at the computer or playing with some other technological equipment or toys, as well as an opportunity to look at the child's ICT-related topic work.
- Displays of children's ICT-related work in the school entrance to inform parents and stimulate their interest.
- Parents being invited to work with groups of children in the classroom.
- Children being able to borrow ICT equipment from the school like calculator games, technical Lego or computer software.
- Parents being offered advice about the software, which could be specifically purchased for use at home.

Excitingly, ICT technology can itself help to forge and maintain productive home–school links. The significance of the possibilities in this area are recognized by a major report recently prepared by The British

Educational Communications and Technology Agency (BECTa) (2001) for the DfES on precisely this topic. This evaluation and research project was based on a survey of 115 schools involved in innovative work developing home–school links in a wide variety of ways. While, of course, many of these schools were at the secondary level, there are already many early years settings, nursery schools and so forth, who have established websites, on which parents and children can access digital photos of the child building their model at school, or playing imaginatively in the sandpit, or whatever is significant at the time. Parents and teachers can email one another, with photos attached. Children without computers at home can take home a laptop with their favourite game loaded on it, so that they can share their enjoyment of it with their parents in the comfort and peace of the home setting. With imagination, the possibilities are endless, and new ideas and technologies will continually emerge (for example, what are the possibilities of WebCam links between home and school, or person-to-person video calls using 3S phones so that child and parent can converse and visually interact during the working day?).

What is clear is that the new technologies have enormous implications not only for what children will learn and need to learn in the new millennium, but also for the ways in which this learning will take place. If they also help to forge stronger links between children's principal carers and educators, they will be making an extremely significant contribution to enhancing the quality of young children's first transitions into formal education, and this can only be highly beneficial.

3
• • •

Responding to the differing needs of children

In determining the most appropriate provisions to be made in early years settings we need to consider the diversity of the children's educational needs. As we noted in Chapter 2, at present there are significant differences in the ICT experiences of individual children as a consequence of access and attitudes. In this chapter we consider this diversity in terms of technological literacy and gender. We also discuss issues of control and empowerment.

The broad issue of access

While technological development progresses at an accelerating rate around the world, and ICTs are now more accessible to young children than ever before, a significant number of young children continue to grow up with little or no access to computers. According to a representative survey of 15,200 9- to 17-year-old children conducted by Unicef in

'I have a lot of information about computers'	26 per cent
'I have some information. . .'	39 per cent
'I have very little information. . .'	21 per cent
'I only know the name'	8 per cent
'I know nothing about it'	6 per cent

Source: Unicef (2001).

2000/01, 35 per cent of children in Europe and Central Asia are still growing up with little or no knowledge of computers and ICT at all.

A recent British survey conducted for the Department for Education and Skills (DfES) (Taylor Nelson Sofres 2002) showed that 74 per cent of parents felt that computers allowed their children to be more creative, and 85 per cent felt that computers made schoolwork more enjoyable for their child. But this really does raise questions about the other 15–26 per cent who did not feel that this was the case. Substantial investment is currently being made by the government into educational ICT but, as we noted in our previous chapter, it is already clear that some children and families will be better placed than others, for both economic and attitudinal reasons, to take advantage of the new opportunities that this opens up for their children. The DfES survey shows that 75 per cent of households with family members in the age range 5–18 years now possess a personal computer, and 64 per cent have internet access. But the 2000 *CensusAt-School* survey (http://www.censusatschool.ntu.ac.uk) shows that parental ICT provision may be significantly different for children in the primary age group and those for secondary. The proportion of households with children in the 0–6 age range with these technologies is therefore likely to be even lower than those with children of 5–10 (primary) age.

Pupils with a mobile phone, access to a computer, or access to the internet

England, Wales and Northern Ireland	Per cent of all pupils	Per cent of primary school pupils	Per cent of high school pupils
With a mobile phone	41.22	16.31	58.89
With access to a computer at home	82.01	78.07	84.80
With access to the internet at home	60.35	54.15	64.74

Source: *CensusAtSchool* (2000).

Of course, access to ICT isn't simply a question of access to computers any more. There are a range of other technologies that may be considered to have significant educational potential such as interactive television (iDTV) and games consoles (although many would argue that this potential has yet to be fully realized). Yet regardless of the specific technology involved, in all of these cases we can't simply take the home ownership of computers as an indicator of early childhood access. Studies do suggest that the children with access in the home tend to benefit more from ICT in school but several studies have identified inequalities of access even within families, based on gender, age and family culture (Facer *et al.* 2000; Furlong *et al.* 2000). We also need to know a good deal more about how the children's individual dispositions towards different kinds of technology are formed. Of households without a computer the DfES survey showed that 31 per cent had an interactive digital television, and 71 per cent had a games console.

Technology with educational potential	*Per cent of households in Autumn 2001*
Interactive digital television	36
DVD player	23
Games console	71
Mobile telephone	88
WAP/3G Phone	8

Source: Taylor Nelson Sofres (2000).

A range of interactive television games have recently been developed for CBeebies, the BBC's new digital television channel for pre-school children. The games feature popular BBC children's characters such as Bill and Ben, Bob the Builder, Noddy, Fireman Sam and the Tweenies.

Perhaps the most obvious question to be considered is whether the wider educational achievements of those children who have less access to technology are being compromised. Software programs are now available to support children's learning in a number of areas of the curriculum. While basic literacy and numeracy skills, letter and number recognition, phonics and counting are the most common, programs are also available that aim to support such diverse areas as creativity, self-expression and problem solving. Given the powerful marketing of these products it is not at all surprising that many parents worry that their children may be disadvantaged if they don't have access to the new technology for these reasons. So do they work? While the evidence is still not entirely clear, it does seem to be the case that some 'programmed learning' packages can be effective in teaching children basic skills. But this is not entirely surprising because we also know that formal, direct (didactic) instructional approaches to early literacy and numeracy are equally effective in teaching children the basic skills at an early stage. The problem is that most early years educators warn against the use of these methods because, despite their effectiveness, the evidence also suggests that their use has other less desirable implications for learning. To put it simply, while we know that we can teach children more basic literacy and numeracy than we do, and we can teach these subjects earlier than we do, we choose not to do so because we know that teaching in this way does little to encourage positive lifelong dispositions to literature and mathematics. Even more seriously, there is a good deal of evidence that teaching the basic skills too early can actually be damaging in terms of these long-term dispositions (Schweinhart and Weikart 1997).

While there is a good deal of research still to be done, there is every reason to suspect that these problems associated with 'hot-housing' young children in the basic literacy and numeracy skills will apply as much to teaching through ICT as in any other way. If children find it 'fun' to learn their letters and numbers with a computer program we must therefore be sure to ask ourselves what it is in particular they are having fun with: is it with the letters and numbers themselves and with reading and mathematics? Or is it with winning the game; achieving a high score; seeing an entertaining animation; or hearing a funny noise? In many cases we may find the software wanting.

According to the Department for Education and Skills (DfES) and to many other authorities on the subject, ICT education is especially important in supporting the development of a 'knowledge economy'. In many of these accounts online service providers are considered to provide a future alternative to the traditional manufacturing industries as a major source of national income. An important implication of this economic shift has already been to accept that the skills that we acquire in schools, colleges and the workplace often become redundant as technology develops. This suggests that a commitment to, and capacity for, 'lifelong' learning will be required of all those individuals who wish to continue to enjoy employment. The argument also suggests that children who learn basic computing skills will adapt more easily to these major changes in the labour market. They will therefore benefit from higher incomes and enjoy wider employment prospects. The country will also benefit from gains in productivity and competitiveness. The core ICT skills that have been identified as especially crucial in all of this are often described as 'new literacies' that are considered 'likely to be as important to individual success and fulfilment as literacy and numeracy have been in the past' (DfES 2002):

'Digital literacy' describes effective information handling, including the ability to:

- identify, locate and retrieve relevant information;
- discern and evaluate;
- access the provenance, reliability and accuracy of information and arguments;
- present in an appropriate style and medium.

'Visual literacy' describes effective interpretation and production of visual imagery, including the ability to:

- translate thinking and creativity into effective presentations;
- manipulate a variety of media, including video;
- appreciate aesthetic values.

(DfES 2002: 11)

In terms of the early years curriculum we can see the foundations of these skills being developed in the children's emerging awareness of a wide range of ICTs seen as providers of different forms (and qualities) of information, and of visual images. These objectives are considered to be best achieved through the children's own playful involvement in the business of obtaining, manipulating and producing information and images.

When considered in these terms, how seriously can we take the moral panic that we sometimes hear about the 'digital divide'? Are young children really disadvantaged for life if they don't gain early experiences of developing these skills? Perhaps the question that we should be asking is how seriously have we, as adults, been disadvantaged by not having these opportunities when we were young? While most of us can remember or appreciate the extended struggles that can be involved in mastering basic literacy and numeracy, does the same apply to ICT? While the successful operation of a computer even a few years ago certainly did involve significant training, applications are now being developed that require little or no training at all. 'Intuitive' design features are increasingly introduced so that there is less need to consult instruction books and manuals, and the operation of the technology becomes simply a matter of 'common sense'.

So what are we arguing here? Are we suggesting that there is little cause for including ICT in early education at all? Certainly not. We are only arguing that the most popular justifications for including ICT in the early years curriculum are sometimes exaggerated. To suggest that children need to play with computers in the early years because they will need to use them when they grow up is to ignore the fact that computer applications are becoming easier and easier to learn. It is also, and this is perhaps even more significant, to ignore the fact that the form that ICTs are going to take when today's infants grow up to be adults is extremely difficult to predict. We only need to think back to the kinds of technologies being used by adults in employment when we were children ourselves to recognize this. How relevant would an education have been if it were based on developing the skills required to apply the technologies used then!

But there are other reasons to consider including ICT in the early years curriculum, and there is another way of considering the issue and relevance of a 'digital divide' in the UK (and other industrialized nations) as well. The digital divide that we should be taking far more seriously than that of 'access' should be the one of 'attitudes'.

The issue of attitudes: gender equality

While many girls have as much access to ICT as do boys in schools, it is significant that they still tend not to choose to take up the ICT opportunities available to them in this field when the time comes for higher education and career choices. Girls make up a very significant group here, but if the future of our economy and the children's future adult careers are really at stake then we should also consider why it is that so many very capable boys also choose to turn their backs on ICT when the opportunities arise.

We have already cited evidence that suggests the parents of secondary age children consider ICT more important than the parents of primary age children. The *CensusAtSchool* data (2000) also shows major regional variations that cannot be ascribed simply to economic factors. In terms of primary age children with mobile telephones for example, 23 per cent of Welsh children reported having them and that is more than twice as many as in London (10 per cent). Yet more of the primary aged children in London had access to computers at home (77 per cent compared with 71 per cent in Wales) and only 45 per cent of the Welsh children had home access to the internet (56 per cent in London). In the home counties 83 per cent of primary age children have access to computers at home and 60 per cent have access to the internet.

From this perspective we can see that it may be technological literacy, or rather a lack of it, that is as much the cause of the digital divide in most industrialized nations as economics. Attitudes may be particularly significant when we consider gender and ICT. Computers are often seen as belonging to the realm of machinery and mathematics, which is, as Wajcman (1991) has noted, a daunting combination for many girls. In fact a number of studies suggest that young girls are less interested in computers (e.g. Siraj-Blatchford and Siraj-Blatchford 2002a). Studies show that even in the nursery children are able to distinguish activities they consider 'appropriate' for their gender, and they react selectively to different toys. Podmore (1991) has shown that children as young as 4 could specify their software preferences and, according to Gourdji (1998), when pre-school children are asked to draw a picture of a child seated next to a computer, the majority of children picture a boy because they say they feel boys are better than girls at computers. As Fletcher-Flinn and Suddendorf (1996) have shown, young children need to see more positive female role models if we are to bridge the computer gender gap.

The equality of opportunity perspective in early years technology has tended to emphasize the importance of supporting girls' access to computers. What has been considered important has been girls having equal opportunity to use the technology. Efforts were made to ensure that girls were given access to the resources (e.g. the computer) even if they chose to play with these resources in a different way from the boys. What this often meant in practice was that, in the case of water play, for example, they could: wash their doll in the water instead of trying to pour water into different containers, or trying out different materials to see if they floated or sank, or seeing how colours mixed in it, and so on. Research by Brooker and Siraj-Blatchford (2002) has also shown that boys and girls play in different ways at the computer. The trouble with this policy of limiting our concern to access is that it doesn't go far enough. While equal opportunities policies are non-sexist they aren't necessarily anti-sexist; they don't concern themselves enough with achieving an equality of *outcomes*. To achieve this we need to do more to challenge the dominant stereotypes, provide 'positive images', and try to change the 'hidden curriculum' of ICT. One possibility to be considered in this is the provision of girls-only times at the computer.

Epstein's (1995) study of children playing with bricks showed girls building elaborate constructions that were subsequently used in their more gendered play with princesses and ponies. This illustrated two things: first (and this was also supported by the evidence and arguments of Valerie Walkerdine (1981) and Bronwyn Davis (1989)), that children are active agents in making their own meanings and in (re)constructing sexism, and second, that educators can, to a greater or lesser degree, shift children's positionings within sexist and heterosexist discourse. Epstein introduced girls-only time in using the bricks in her infant classroom. In this particular case, the girls' ability to challenge (both for themselves and for the boys) gendered stereotypes was made possible precisely because they were able to occupy contradictory positions at the same time, playing with the boys' toys while taking up feminine subject positions.

Brooker and Siraj-Blatchford's (2002) study of how 3- and 4-year-olds experience the nursery computer provided similar findings, with the girls often extending their socio-dramatic play beyond the screen; 'grabbing' apples and pears from the screen, begging each other to share them, and licking their lips appreciatively after pretending to eat them. So 'girls-only' time may be worth considering. But while some research has found that girls learn significantly more when the software they are applying is gender-neutral, rather than male-oriented (Littleton *et al.* 1998), the argument that is sometimes made, that we should be providing girls with more feminine video games or other software, is more problematic. This suggestion, that the major problem to be solved is the paucity of feminine software, is based upon the observation that children who use video games tend to go on to make more use of computers for other purposes. This argument has also been extended to suggest that this has increased their confidence with the technology sufficiently to encourage an interest in a technological career (Cassell 1999).

It is certainly the case that computer games engage children's interest, and young children often persevere with a game for extended periods. This is one of the real strengths of the computer game format. The one feature of these kinds of games that we have noticed nearly every time we have used them with young children is how involved some of the children become in the story. The most successful of games become like well-loved books. The children want to play them again and again. The suggestion that children who get 'hooked' on video games may therefore go on to take a more general interest in technology seems plausible, but evidence also suggests that when girls do take an interest in technology they are often harassed by boys who seem to have a need to define their masculinity in direct opposition to the girls' femininity that is defined in technological terms (Epstein 1995). There is also some reason to be concerned about the quality of some of the software titles that have been produced for girls in the past. Manufacturers certainly need to be careful that when games or any other ICT applications are 'feminized' they don't lose the essential elements that made them educationally worthwhile in the first place.

As Brenda Laurel in her research for *Interval Research* and *Purple Moon* found, girls also dislike many of the features typically found in computer games: the strong emphasis on hand–eye coordination; repetitive action; scoring points; and time pressure (Laurel 1990). Research with older children has shown that boys and girls have different video game preferences, with boys tending to enjoy programs that have leading characters that are fantasy-based action heroes with 'super' abilities inhabiting larger-than-life settings. They like games where the major goal is to win, and the play is linear. These are games where speed and action are crucial and the outcomes are clear cut, with one 'correct' solution. Girls, by contrast, enjoy video game adventures where the leading characters are everyday people that they can relate to and where the major goal is to explore, with degrees of success and outcome. They also like games of discovery with strong 'realistic' story lines where success comes through collaboration and the development of friendships. For Laurel, the problem of 'pink software' such as the Barbie programs is that while they may initially catch the girls' attention they do little to engage and empower them to use the technology, or arouse their intellectual curiosity.

As Thouvenelle et al. (1994) have also suggested, there are therefore a number of things that educators can do to support girls. They can:

- consider girls' interests and interaction styles when selecting and evaluating software for classroom use;
- model the use of the computer as a learning and productivity tool and invite children, especially girls, to observe and assist them in the work; and
- promote equity by offering special times for 'girls only' use of computers, which permits girls to explore the computer without having to directly compete with boys.

(Thouvenelle et al. 1994)

But as previously noted, it is not just the girls that we should be concerned about in this context. We should also consider the attitudes of many young boys towards technology. Margaret Cox (1997) cites Offir's (1993) study of 60 pre-school children which showed that children with a good self-image had more positive attitudes towards computers than those with a low self-image. Cox argues that children's motivations towards computing are influenced by a number of factors including the regularity of use, their experience of failure, their fear of failure and self-image.

We have argued here that the digital divide is not just about access, and, we have also argued that it is not just about encouraging children to develop any particular new 'skills' either. In Chapter 1 we argued for an ICT education emphasizing technological literacy and this is consistent with the Curriculum Guidance for the Foundation Stage (CGFS) (QCA/DfEE 2000). Children need to learn about new technology and they need to develop an emerging critical awareness of the technological choices that they make themselves, and the choices that the adults around them make as well. Technological literacy encompasses digital literacy and visual literacy and, as we shall see, it includes the development of an awareness of control technology as well. But this is not the only sense in which we should be considering control.

The issue of control

There are many examples in psychological research of tasks where being in control has turned out to be crucial for effective learning. Guha (1987) cites, for example, experiments concerned with visual learning in which subjects are required to wear 'goggles' which make everything look upside down. They are then required to sit in a wheelchair and learn to move safely through an environment. The results of such experiments show that subjects moving themselves around the environment (and having a lot of initial 'crashes') learn to do this much more quickly than those who are wheeled safely about by an adult helper. The parallels here with Bruner's 'play' and 'taught' groups, as reviewed in the previous chapter, are striking.

This issue of control also relates strongly to two further important ideas in children's learning, namely responsiveness and confidence. We have all experienced the young infant who delights in repetitive play, throwing an object on the floor for an adult to pick up, over and over again, with the child's glee becoming more and more unbounded (unlike the adult's). It has been very clearly established from a whole range of research (originally responding to Bowlby's work on child care) that young children flourish best when their adult carers are responsive and where their experience is consistent and predictable (Schaffer 1977). This same principle was demonstrated quite a long time ago by an unexpected finding from Watson and Ramey's (1972) 'contingency mobile' experiment. This involved families with eight-week-old infants using a special cot on to which was joined a mobile. Where the mobile moved it proved to be no more interesting to the infants than if it stayed still. However, if the mobile moved when the infant pressed down on the pillow, this became hugely fascinating and the research team had some difficulty in retrieving their apparatus at the end of the experiment! These infants were in control and their parents could see for themselves the huge benefits this brought to their child's well-being.

What emerges from a wide range of research over the past twenty to thirty years, therefore, is that children learn to be confident and flexible thinkers when they grow up in an environment which is responsive and consistent, and which encourages them to be playful. They need to be in control of their own learning and will learn most powerfully through tackling real and meaningful problems in their own ways, rather than by being 'taught' set procedures. Because of the responsive and interactive nature of much ICT technology, the electronic toy or the computer is itself capable of providing feedback, help and support to children. While they may still need some guidance occasionally from the teacher, this need is often much reduced by the use of computer software, for example, which can react contingently dependent upon the child's behaviour (a feature which also, of course, makes playing games highly motivating). This strongly supports the child's sense of being in control, and of independence in his or her learning. It is clearly important for the teacher to be sensitive to these issues; in relation to graphics, or programmable toys, or adventures and simulations, this also implies allowing children on occasions to set their own challenges and to tackle them in their own way, just as we would with the building bricks, or the sandpit, or the cutting and sticking table. Furthermore, as we shall see in later chapters, an increasingly common feature of advanced electronic toys and computer games is that they are capable of 'learning' in some simple form themselves. This is a potentially very exciting development because it makes learning explicit in ways which have also been shown to be very powerful in encouraging children to learn how to learn and become independent learners.

While the educational benefits to young children of problem-solving activities, and more open-ended approaches that put them in control of their own learning, are widely recognized, organizing them effectively with young children can be difficult. Many educators find this kind of approach difficult to organize and manage within the classroom. Inspection reports often show, for example, that areas concerned with specific content are taught well, but that areas concerned with using and applying subjects, or developing skills and processes, cause educators more difficulty. Some of the key difficulties which early years educators experience in this area are as follows:

- for problem solving to be worthwhile, it has to be challenging, so that children often require fairly intensive help from a highly skilled educator;
- children's approaches to problems are inevitably varied; and the sheer variety of directions and activities embarked upon may be difficult to manage and resource;
- open-ended problem-solving approaches are difficult to timetable; the time that is taken to carry out particular tasks can be highly

unpredictable, and it is often difficult and educationally disadvanta-geous to stop quickly in the middle of a particular part of the process;
- problem solving is often about trying out ideas and seeing if they work; through lack of experience children can therefore sometimes pursue ideas which are doomed to failure for a long time, and then experience severe disappointment when the moment of truth arrives after all their hard work;
- because solving problems requires hard work and commitment from the children, to be effective problems have to engage their interests and imaginations; 'off-the-peg' problems often suffer as a result in com-parison with spontaneously devised 'real' problems; the latter, how-ever, require a huge organizational and imaginative effort from the educator – while many able educators manage to create these kinds of authentic opportunities (see, for example, Atkinson (1992) in the area of mathematics and Fisher (1987) for examples across the curriculum), it is not something which is easy to sustain as a very regular part of their provision.

The use of computer-based games and problem-solving activities alleviates a number of these difficulties. A *well-designed* computer game provides children with immediate feedback, with consistency and with the opportunities for repetition that they need to build their skills and confidence as learners.

Further, in well-designed games, a good variety of possible responses by the children are catered for and dealt with appropriately. The range of responses permitted by different games is, in fact, an interesting issue to which we shall return in later chapters. Games vary from the simplest, aimed at the youngest children, where very constrained 'yes/no' type choices are offered and only one response is allowed (any other response produces either nothing or a message saying something like 'Oh yes, you do!') to the most complex where the child types in messages and the com-puter is able to respond to a reasonably large vocabulary, where several possible decisions can be made at any time and, in some cases, where problems can be solved in a variety of ways. From a negative perspective this 'prescribed' feature of possible solutions in, for example, some simu-lations and adventure games can be criticized for limiting children's creativity. More positively, however, it can be seen as a supportive feature which enables the teacher using interactive stories, simulations and games to provide children with a progression in level of difficulty. As we will see below, there are also plenty of opportunities for children to be engaged in more open-ended activities away from the computer that have been stimulated by the exciting challenges posed within these kinds of games.

The difficulties of timetabling problem-solving activities are to some extent also alleviated by well-designed computer games. When children finish a particular session on the computer they are not faced with the problems of clearing up the debris or storing their half-finished construction and the pieces that are half-made. When they resume, also, they do not have to remember what they have done and which point they have reached. They do not have to find all their bits and pieces from the last time and redo the bit that has got lost or squashed. Some games even allow individual 'adventures-so-far' to be saved at any point and returned to at a later date. In terms of thinking time, computer games are very efficient. When children are working with a computer game, they will spend the vast majority of that time working on the problems posed by the game, not wandering around looking for the glue. We wouldn't wish to imply for a moment that more practical types of problem solving are not worth doing. Far from it. They are clearly an important element in any child's educational diet and offer experiences which cannot be simulated on a computer. But it is important to recognize the different but equally valuable experience computer-based problems can offer.

The fourth area of management difficulty relates to the trial and error nature of much problem solving. One of the present authors was first alerted to the particular strength of computers in this area when working with young children using a computer graphics program. At the press of a key, children could rub out anything they didn't like (and without making a nasty smudge or a hole in the paper!), change the thickness of a line, or the colour of a shape, and so on. The opportunities for experimentation were boundless in a way that paint or chalk or crayon cannot really offer to a young child. The same is very much the case with problem solving. In an adventure game or simulation, for example, you can try out one possibility, see that it doesn't work, and try out another, all in a matter of moments. In real practical problem solving in mathematics or science or design technology it is very much more difficult to provide for this kind of trial and error learning with young children. In practical work children can very easily spend a lot of time and effort on an idea before it becomes clear to them that it will not work. In an adventure game probably the worst that can happen is that you are splatted by the aliens, or eaten by the wicked witch, but you always miraculously survive to have another go, and you have learned what not to do the next time!

4

Programmable toys and control technology

The 'control technology' part of the ICT curriculum has often been mis-understood to be a highly gendered set of activities involving complex Legofi-Technic construction kits of cranes or ski-lifts or some such, various fancy bits of electronics and the ability to write computer programs in unfathomable binary codes. In fact, in many schools and increasingly in early years settings, control technology activities are taking place which bear no resemblance to this stereotype. It is the intention of this chapter to explore some of the exciting activities and experiences in which we can appropriately engage young children in this area.

We would want to argue that there are at least three very fundamental reasons, closely related to themes already introduced earlier in this book, why control technology should be a significant part of young children's ICT experience. These reasons relate to children's learning about ICT technology and computers, and also to their developing skills more generally as learners, thinkers and problem solvers. To begin with, as we have discussed in Chapter 1 and elsewhere, it is a large and important part of the Foundation Stage curriculum to help children to become aware of technology around them, in their homes and their local environments. When you construct a list of this technology, it quickly becomes clear that many everyday applications of computer technology are concerned with a control function – for example, in a washing machine or a microwave oven, in traffic lights, remote controls for TV, stereo systems etc., in your car, in burglar alarms, in your camera, and so on. In an increasing multiplicity of circumstances, we are using small computers or micro-processors to control what happens, and it is an important part of young children's education to become aware of, and to develop an understanding of, this kind of technology.

Second, engaging in control technology activities obliges children to deal with and to construct simple computer 'programs'. As we have also discussed in Chapter 1, these are, of course, a fundamental feature of every kind of ICT and computer technology, but their role and effect is perhaps most clearly evident in control applications, where you can very directly observe the consequences of particular parts of the program, and of making changes to programs. In this sense, control technology experiences give young children their most profound insights into modern ICT, and help to demystify it and make it transparent.

Third, and finally, as we have seen in Chapter 3, a good range of psychological evidence suggests control technology activities and experiences may help children to develop their more general abilities to think and to learn. It is this third area that we want to focus on in this chapter. Children learn most effectively when they are in control of their own learning and when they are allowed and encouraged to be playful. As we shall see, control technology activities lend themselves powerfully to this style of learning.

Planning

Another major advantage of control programs involves the construction of sequences of commands, and this obliges children to plan. As has long been recognized within developmental psychology (see, for example, Miller *et al.* 1960), the ability to plan is a fundamental and probably unique characteristic of human thinking. It is also an ability which emerges early. Judy De Loache and Ann Brown (1987) have elegantly revealed the early emergence of planning skills among young children.

The most ambitious claims as regards involving children in constructing or writing programs and the development of learning and thinking skills were, of course, made by Seymour Papert (1981) in his classic book *Mindstorms: Children, Computers and Powerful Ideas*. In this, among other things, he claimed that his programmable 'turtle' and the programming language LOGO, which he invented for children to use, gave children 'an object to think with' (1981: 11). More particularly, he argued that the experience of constructing programs of instructions helped children's thinking in a number of ways, which he termed his 'powerful ideas'.

These have been usefully summarized by Underwood and Underwood (1990) as follows:

1 Programming requires rigorous thinking to be made explicit. There is no 'fudge button' when it comes to giving instructions about the movement of the cursor (the screen version of the turtle, or indeed the robot turtle itself) – it moves exactly as instructed and makes no assumptions of its own. Imprecise instructions are not recognized, and reformulations are demanded.

2 Programming provides an environment in which the general concepts of transformation, function and variable can be used and their consequences seen. These powerful abstract concepts can be seen in operation through programs, and LOGO programs are particularly valuable on account of their graphical output. LOGO programs can be seen to make thinking visible.

3 With problem solving through programming, it is possible to appreciate the usefulness of heuristic approaches to a solution. These are the general problem-solving skills involved in planning the route to a solution, solving problems by breaking them into smaller parts, and solving problems by analogy. In particular, programming can foster the idea that problem solving can be organized by parts. Small procedures can be seen as the building blocks from which large solutions are derived.

4 The interactive process of getting a program to run as intended gives an appreciation of debugging an imperfect solution. Errors can be helpful, in that the nature of errors can be informative as a diagnostic in locating the problem. This strategy of using errors as the starting point for improvement can be generalized to other problem-solving tasks.

5 The vocabulary of programming, and the necessity to openly discuss the process of problem solving during programming, give an awareness of the process of problem solving. This reflectivity of thought gives strength to the control processes which are necessary in the selection between alternative routes to a solution, and in the reviewing of resources necessary for problem solving. This awareness of process has also been called metacognition – knowledge about our own personal cognitive processes, their limitations and their application. Awareness of our ability to handle problems includes knowledge of the ways in which we know ourselves capable of solving and knowledge of the kinds of activities in which we must engage in order to find a solution. An important part of this awareness of problem-solving strategies is knowledge

that individual problems call for individual solutions. The selection of the most appropriate solution will depend upon a cost/benefit analysis of the alternatives.

(Underwood and Underwood 1990: 36–7)

Underwood and Underwood (1990) go on to review in some detail research evidence which has both supported and questioned Papert's claims for LOGO. There are, of course, difficulties with this kind of research, because studies are mostly based on the effects of relatively short periods of exposure for the children, and the development of the kinds of generalized cognitive abilities discussed by Papert is notoriously difficult to establish. However, there are studies where clear evidence has emerged of more specific gains among quite young children.

Lawler (1985), for example, reported the results of exposing his 6-year-old daughter Miriam to an intensive six-month period of working with LOGO. She clearly developed problem-solving, planning and debugging skills of a very high order, well beyond what would be expected of the average child of her age. She also showed evidence of transferring ways of thinking about problems to off-computer activities, for example, analysing her father's attempts at skipping in terms of 'bugs' – the 'too soon' bug, when he jumped too early, and the 'too low' bug when he didn't jump high enough. In another more straightforwardly experimental study, Clements and Gullo (1984) involved 6-year-olds in LOGO activities over a period of three months. They pre- and post-tested the children on a range of cognitive ability tests and found gains on the Torrance Test of Creative Thinking and on a test of reflectivity which were not matched by a non-LOGO control group. They also found differences in favour of the LOGO group on post-tests of metacognition (in which the children indicated when they had sufficient information to solve a particular problem) and of verbally describing a route from a map.

As Underwood and Underwood (1990) report, however, there are other studies where no such gains have appeared as a result of LOGO-type experiences, although even where there have been no measurable cognitive gains, there is often clear evidence of the children's enjoyment of and involvement in these kinds of activities, which appear to be highly motivating for young children. The lesson here would appear to be, therefore, that one should not expect large and generalized developments of cognitive abilities over relatively short periods of time, and as a consequence of relatively specific experiences. While programming sequences of instructions on computers may not be the magical key to unlock children's brain power that Papert appeared to claim, nevertheless, what evidence we have suggests that appropriate control technology experiences for young children can help their thinking develop in specific ways and make some important contributions. These contributions are likely to be towards developing:

- positive attitudes towards problem solving and errors;
- accuracy of verbal instructions;
- planning abilities; and
- metacognitive understandings about their own learning.

In the remainder of this chapter we want to look at the kinds of activities which seem likely to foster these developments in young children most effectively. Before doing so, however, it is worth reflecting on some general characteristics of activities which are likely to enhance the quality of young children's learning in this area. In relation to control technology activities, the key elements which we always need to have very much at the forefront of our thinking are control itself, playfulness, and relevance and meaning. In their review of the research, Underwood and Underwood (1990) concluded importantly that open-ended activities, which put the children in control and allowed for a playful, trial and error approach, were consistently the most successful in terms of enhancing children's thinking. Other researchers in the area have also emphasized this element, as well as the significance of placing control activities within meaningful contexts. For example, Carol Fine and Mary Lou Thornbury (2000), as we shall see in a moment, have carried out exciting work with programmable toys and have argued very powerfully for the practice of placing control activities in story or narrative settings. In this regard the arguments are very similar to those which we develop later in Chapter 5 in relation to computer simulations and adventure games for young children. As in so many other areas, if we can engage the power of young children's imaginations then the benefits to their involvement and to their understanding are enormous.

Bearing these general principles in mind, we want to look at introductory control activities, at electronic and relational toys, at programmable toys and finally at computer control programs and examine in turn how each of these can best be used with young children to enhance the kind of learning we have discussed. In these four kinds of control technology activities there is clearly some kind of a progression. Young children will be more able to exploit the possibilities of computer control programmes if they have had some of the other experiences previously. However, in our experience, games can and will be developed by children in each of these areas to which they will want to return even when they are capable of managing the more sophisticated technology, and this variety of experience should be encouraged.

Introductory control activities

Young children will benefit from introductory control activities of two kinds. First they need to develop a familiarity and confidence with all kinds of technological devices which have a control element. It is fundamental that in any good quality, well-resourced early years setting, there should be as wide a range as possible of such devices to which the children have access (although they will clearly benefit from adult support with many pieces of technology, and for health and safety reasons this may often also be advisable). These devices can be technologically simple, so that they can just be turned on and off (e.g. a torch); they might contain a few alternatives or programs (e.g. a toaster, a microwave, a fridge, a simple camera, or a washing machine); or they might be more complicated with a range of functions and values or choices (e.g. a photocopier, a cassette recorder, a television or radio). A judicious mixture of open-ended and more structured tasks needs to be provided, with plenty of opportunity for free play.

Structured tasks need to be devised which have a clear purpose from the children's point of view, but which require the children to practise using the various control functions. A good example of such an activity with a tape recorder, for example, is where a story or a recipe has been pre-recorded on a tape. The children are required to listen to each page of the story, or instruction in the recipe, and then turn off or pause the tape while they turn the page/look at the pictures or carry out that part of the recipe. Then they turn the tape on again, and so on.

One of the requirements of the Foundation Stage Curriculum Guidance is that children are helped to understand how things work by disassembling them, and a useful experience at this early stage can be for children to be shown how to remove and insert batteries into simple toys or devices (e.g. an electronic toy, toothbrush or torch) and examine the consequences. Another important point is that parents can clearly be very usefully involved in these introductory activities, being encouraged to provide their children with experiences of technology in the environment (pushing the button at the pedestrian crossing or on granny's front door) and in the home.

The second kind of introductory control activity is concerned with introducing young children to the idea of a program or set of instructions. There are all kinds of opportunities and games that can be played here. Cooking recipes are an obvious example. Sequencing games and puzzles – for example, putting pictures from a story in the correct order and retelling the story holding up the cards in turn – are also valuable here. As many of the control activities which will be on offer later involve moving an object or person around an environment, games based on this idea are also valuable. For example, an adult can be blindfolded and instructed by the children how to walk across the room to reach a particular target location. This can also be done with the children themselves being directed, but then they will often feel safest if they have a large bag over their heads so they cannot see where they are going, but can still see their feet. They will need lots of practice at listening and following precisely as well as giving precise instructions. A favourite and very safe game here is where you all sit on chairs in a circle and children take turns to be directed to find a friend. Toys and puppets can also be given directions, and here there are lots of opportunities for using a story context (e.g. Incy Wincy Spider climbing up the spout, or Red Riding Hood trying to avoid the big bad wolf and get to Grandma's house).

Electronic and relational toys

There are a whole range of electronic toys available, many of which offer young children valuable control technology experiences. These toys currently seem to fall into three categories, each of which offers a different experience or set of possibilities. First, there are electronic toy versions of pieces of technology which are perhaps too expensive or sophisticated to have a real working example in an early years educational setting. A good example of this currently is the electronic cash register from the Early Learning Centre. This is reviewed on the Foundation Stage page of the website of Framlingham Sir Robert Hitcham's Primary School in Suffolk (www.hitchams.suffolk.sch.uk/foundation):

> The children loved playing with this item especially within the context of the role-play area. They soon learnt that it would only work if they pressed the 'on' button and that they had to press the 'open' button in order for the drawer to open. A few of the more able children, with adult support, were beginning to use it to make very simple additions, but they found it difficult to remember to always press the cancel button before trying another calculation . . . It is quite robust and withstood being dropped on the floor accidentally a few times. The addition of a credit card swipe made the product very realistic especially with the accompanying sound, but it was a pity that the use of this function didn't enable the till drawer to open, as in real life, as the children didn't know what to do when they had swiped the card and nothing happened . . .

As can be seen from this review, a real working cash machine might be better in some respects, but if one cannot be obtained, then this toy version, readily available and for relatively little expense, certainly offers some valuable play experiences and perhaps has the merit of simplifying what is a rather complex piece of technology in a way which makes it usable by young children. Another toy checkout unit possibility currently available, and well worth investigating, is the Playskool Store marketed by Hasbro. This unit actually clips onto the computer keyboard and provides a point of sale shopping simulation on-screen that incorporates a working till and bar-code reader.

There are other electronic toy versions of a range of technological devices on the market, for example, mobile phones, video cameras and so on. Before purchasing these for early years settings, however, we need to ask ourselves why we are not providing the real item, and whether the toy version provides useful and realistic functionality that will provide the children with technologically valid experiences, or with valuable play opportunities.

Another useful example in this category are toy versions of control systems that incorporate sensing devices. Many control systems in the real world, of course, incorporate devices which sense changes in the environment, which then trigger particular actions, e.g. burglar alarms, central heating systems, fuel injection systems in cars and so on. Lego Mybot is currently perhaps the best example of this kind of technology presented in a way which is appropriate for young children (see Figure 4.1). This uses Lego plus 'intelligent bricks' for the children to build up and make their own interactive robots or cars or planes or

Figure 4.1   Lego Mybot

whatever their imagination allows. The three 'intelligent bricks' provided comprise a petrol pump (which detects the passing of time), an alarm system (which is a motion detector) and a light-sensitive brick. Each combination of identity and activity bricks brings up a different cockpit screen. The display is interactive, too – it changes depending on the way the children move the MyBot. With the aeroplane brick, the display shows the changing horizon line, and with the car brick, a speedometer comes up. The fact that the bricks provided interlink with standard Lego and Duplo bricks means that young children can incorporate the Mybot bricks into their own designs. In our experience, this is a very popular toy with young children and one from which a good deal of technological learning is possible.

The second kind of electronic toy is the remote control vehicle and here again perhaps the best example currently available is the Lego Action Wheelers Remote Control (see Figure 4.2), for the simple reason that standard Lego and Duplo bricks can be built onto it, so that children can develop their own vehicle designs. You can even build it onto the Mybot bricks (or vice versa). As with most remote control cars, it has buttons to control left and right turns and both of these can be pressed to go forward or back. This is, of course, very popular with young children. In our experience, and that of others, it takes children a little practice to learn to control these kinds of cars, but they enjoy the challenge and are successful more quickly than you might anticipate. All kinds of games can be devised involving following set routes, getting out of mazes, and even having races – two sets can be used as you can set different frequencies.

Figure 4.2 Lego Action Wheelers Remote Control

Courses can often be most conveniently constructed using the kinds of large building blocks that are present in most early years settings. Clearly the children are learning a good deal about directions, distances, fine motor control and building up sequences of actions to construct a route, and all in a very motivating context. Both Mybot and Lego Action Wheelers Remote Control are reviewed on the Framlingham Sir Robert Hitcham's Primary School website.

The third kind of electronic toy which offers valuable learning opportunities for young children is what has become known as the 'relational' or robotic toy. These are toys that have been recently introduced mostly onto the domestic market and include Furbies, Tamagotchies, and robotic puppies such as Techno and Aibo (see Figure 4.3). They are termed 'relational' because they present themselves as having emotional states and so young children (and many adults!) find themselves engaging in pleasurable emotional interactions with these toys. This in itself presents opportunities in terms of 'emotional literacy' within the PSHE curriculum, but from an educational point of view perhaps the even more interesting feature of these toys is that they are increasingly being designed to mature and to learn. Techno and Aibo, for example, learn new language (e.g. their name!) and movements from their interactions with children.

These toys are potentially very exciting because they present to children simplified examples of other beings who apparently feel emotions and think and learn. This connects very powerfully with two key developments in children's psychological development, namely their developing 'theory of mind' and their developing 'metacognition'. The first refers to their understanding that other beings have their own minds, with their

Poo-Chi Blue

Figure 4.3 Relational toys

own feelings, knowledge and perspectives (see Mitchell (1997) for an introduction). The most widely accepted current theory is that this understanding is fundamental to the formation of social relationships. Sufferers from autism appear to lack the ability to form a 'theory of mind'. Early experiments in providing 4- and 5-year-olds with improvised closed circuit television (CCTV) systems (Siraj-Blatchford and Siraj-Blatchford 2002a) suggests that they may encourage increased communication and collaboration and this could be developmentally significant. 'Metacognition' refers to children's developing understandings about their own mental processing or cognition. A considerable body of evidence within developmental psychology has established that metacognitive abilities are crucially responsible for children's development of the abilities to think and learn (see Robinson 1983). As well as potentially giving children a new and helpful perspective on emotional states and on the processes of learning, relational toys are also, of course, highly motivating toys and ones which powerfully exemplify the processes of control technology. What children learn overall is precisely how the toy reacts to their own different actions and words and thus how to control the toy and its development.

Programmable toys

The next stage on is clearly the programmable toy. These are distinguishable because, whereas the electronic toys we have discussed in the previous section respond to individual instructions or actions, with programmable toys a whole sequence of instructions can be input, remembered and acted upon as a sequence or program. There are a whole range of these kinds of toys available, but perhaps the mostly widely used currently with young children are the Pixie (see Figure 4.4) and Pip from Swallow Systems and the Roamer from Valiant Technology. All of these have been designed so that they are a basic control box which the children can dress up to make into any character they want. They do differ, however, in the sophistication of their controls and the range of their possible actions.

The simplest of the three is Pixie. Very useful reviews of its functions and educational uses can be found on the Swallow Systems website (www.swallow.co.uk), the Framlingham Sir Robert Hitcham's Primary School website mentioned above and the DATEC website http://www-DATEC.educ.cam.ac.uk

There are, of course, enormous advantages in Pixie's simplicity. In order to use it, you do not have to be able to recognize number symbols,

Figure 4.4 Programmable toy: Pixie

but you do have to be able to count! A turn is always a right angle (whereas on Roamer you can give precise angles). Because of this simplicity it is not possible to generate a 'syntax error' or impossible command. Another very useful feature is that once a program is running all the keys are 'panic' buttons that will stop Pixie if they are pressed – very useful to stop it plunging to its death or disappearing irretrievably under the cupboard.

On all of the websites mentioned, and many others, there are lots of ideas for using Pixie. Here, for example, is an idea from the Swallows system website:

> PIXIE is typically used on a table top. Most often it will run over a 'microworld' made by sticking pictures, coloured spots or letters onto a large sheet of paper or cardboard. The microworld makes a background for the activities of the children. Thus, if the microworld is a map of some streets, the children could be asked to program PIXIE to behave as the school bus, going along the streets and pausing at the bus stops to collect children before finally ending up at school. The microworld gives the teacher a consistent environment in which to use PIXIE and ensures that the same program will give consistent results.

There are also ideas for dressing Pixie up as various characters from well-loved stories, as a frog who can bound from leaf to leaf, or the ultimate dressing up experience of the fashion show, with the children programming Pixie to strut his/her stuff on the catwalk! There are downloadable resources from the Swallows System website to help with all these ideas, including a blank Pixie cover for the children to create their own designs (either by hand, or within a paint/graphics computer application, which has the advantage that these designs can then be emailed back for display on the website).

As we have discussed earlier, setting control activities in the context of a story can be very effective. Joyce Fields (1991) has reported some very exciting work based on the story of a Concept Keyboard package called *Jemima's Journey* about the adventures of a wild duck. As part of this she recounts a very successful series of activities where the children dressed up a LOGO turtle to represent Jemima and attempted to recreate her journey from the barn, around the yard, out of the gate, across the road and over to the pond. The well-loved stories of *Rosie's Walk*, or *Going on a Bear Hunt*, or *Three Little Pigs* would all clearly offer similar opportunities, and there are many more such stories. Pixie and Pip, being rectangular, can easily be transformed into lorries or trucks, and tasks can be set which involve delivering items to different locations (Bob the Builder delivering his bricks?).

Because of the need to direct programmable toys to travel specific distances or to turn by a set amount, a number of games can be played which enhance the counting element of this activity. All kinds of board games and races, perhaps using dice, can be made. Ruth Pimentel has constructed all kinds of stimulating ideas for using Pixie, many of which are in a special section of the Swallow Systems website.

What is overwhelmingly important, however, is to allow the children to self-initiate activities with programmable toys. Fine and Thornbury recount their experiences of working with Pip in a nursery class:

> The children in the nursery were using a robust robot called 'Pip'. Their theme for the half-term was the family life of Mr and Mrs Wolf. The Pips were dressed up with masks and the first day was divided between experimenting with the robot and transforming it into a character by dressing it up. For a few days different groups explored a route to the shops or a route to pick up Baby Wolf from school . . . after the initial introduction of the robot, the children took ownership of the Pip activities, using two Pips in a game of chase or a race.
>
> (Fine and Thornbury 2000: 127)

Once the children have been shown some basic possibilities, they will develop their own ideas, and we know that, as we have discussed elsewhere, allowing the children to take control of their own learning in this way will always be the most effective, at least partly because children will set their own challenges. One of the present authors has the experience of introducing the idea of Roamer skittles to a group of 3- and 4-year-olds in a nursery school. Whereas this was introduced as a challenge to program Roamer to hit a whole set of skittles, within a few days the children were seeing if they could knock down one skittle from increasingly long distances and with obstacles blocking the way. In all this enthusiastic activity, of course, the children were continuously enhancing their abilities to plan, to learn from and debug errors, to discuss using precise and mathematical language, and to construct simple computer programs, giving themselves powerful insights into the fundamentals of control technology.

On-screen control programs

The final apparent progression within control technology is to move to working on a computer screen. There is, for example, a Pip simulator marketed by Swallow Systems which allows children to carry out some simple Pip activities on screen (see Figure 4.5). The simulator has all the Pip buttons plus extra buttons for loading and saving programs, setting a target to aim at and printing the program out. As the buttons are pressed the program appears in text at the top right. When the 'Go' button is pressed an icon moves around the main area to the left to execute the instructions. The instruction being executed is highlighted in the text area as it is executed. The icon leaves a trail to show its path.

Within the age group with which we are concerned this last feature provides perhaps the only clear advantage of this 2D simulated screen

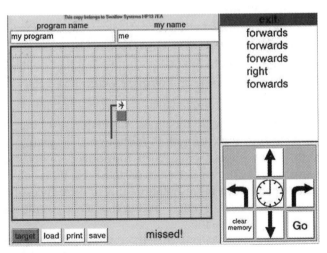

Figure 4.5 Pip simulator

Figure 4.6   Ben and Nathan's LOGO picture

version over the 3D Pixie that works in the real environment. One can attach a felt tip pen to Pixie, or any of the other programmable toys, to leave a trail, but in practice it is quite difficult to get this to work well. Bennett (1997) does provide a good example of a useful application of this facility in terms of encouraging children to draw pictures with a basic LOGO program (see Figure 4.6). What this illustrates well is the way in which control technology activities can engage children in very productive collaborative problem solving:

> Two 6-year-olds, Ben and Nathan, were using LOGO to draw a tree to go with their picture of a house. They were experiencing difficulty getting the size right.
>
> *Ben:*   Try 100.
> *Nathan:* That's no good. It's bigger.
> *Ben:*   What was it . . . how big?
> *Nathan:* Err . . . 70, I think.
> *Ben:*   Shall we try 70 again?
> *Nathan:* Yes, all right. [*Types in.*]
> *Ben:*   Yeh. It *is* too big.
> *Nathan:* We could try 50, that's smaller.
> *Ben:*   Yeh or 47, that's smaller.
> *Nathan:* Or 40 anything.
> *Ben:*   Do 47. [*Nathan types in 47.*] Yeh, that's better.
>
> Nathan is considered to be of average ability and Ben receives additional help with reading and number work.
>
> (Bennett 1997: 39)

Working on the screen with the Pixie simulator also introduces the children to recording their programs (although it is vitally important, of course, that they should have been introduced to recording them pictorially or iconically during activities with the real Pixie before this). As with any computer screen representation, it also introduces the children to 2D representations of 3D events – and in this sense having a simulator of a real object is a useful facility.

What is apparent, however, is that the computer screen version has some severe limitations and disadvantages for the young child. Pixie can no longer be dressed up to be a character in a story, and the environment in which he moves is now just an arid set of squares on a screen. With the Pixie simulator you can only play one game which is pre-programmed into the software. Children's creativity in inventing their own worlds, environments, stories, adventures and games to play with a progammable toy within is all largely unsupported and untapped by this form of the activity.

There are other on-screen versions of programmable vehicles which make some attempts to overcome some of these limitations. Three worth mentioning here are the *2go* program within the 2Simple suite marketed by 2Simple Software; the Jelly Bean Hunt in *Trudy's Time and Place House* by Edmark; and *Thomas the Clown* by Logotron. *2go* offers four levels of control panels, beginning with something very similar to Pixie and progressing on to something similar to Roamer. It also offers the opportunity to move the cursor around different background environments – a race track, a town, planets in space, islands in a sea and flowers in a garden are provided – and to change the cursor to an appropriate vehicle or animal in each case (see Figure 4.7). Other backgrounds can also very easily be imported (although, sadly, the cursor cannot be changed beyond the pre-programmed options). There is also, usefully, the option to have a grid either displayed or not. In a number of important ways *2go* is therefore more flexible and more open-ended, but clearly has limitations compared to working with real programmables. Curiously, also, the option to input a series of moves and record them as a program is only available at the highest level.

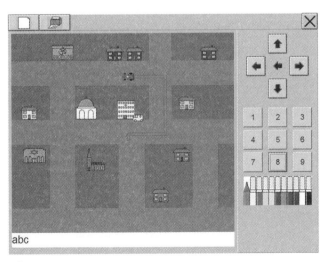

Figure 4.7 *2go*

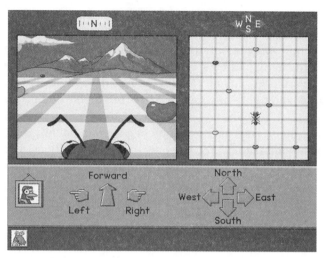

Figure 4.8 The Jelly Bean Hunt in *Trudy's Time and Place House*

A characteristic of all these kinds of basic on-screen programmable vehicle type programs is that the environment in which the vehicle or animal moves is presented from above as a map. While this might be a useful introduction, in some ways, to this version of 2D representations of the world, it is one which causes some difficulties for young children. The Jelly Bean Hunt in *Trudy's Time and Place House* (see Figure 4.8) is worthy of note if only because it presents both the worm's eye and bird's eye view simultaneously, which may well help children to begin to develop their understandings of these various representations.

Thomas the Clown moves further away from simply simulating a 3D progammable toy kind of environment, and in this sense does offer something rather different. Here the children are engaged in control activities on screen, but the environments and the vehicles involved are presented much more 'realistically' and are much more richly animated, that is, there is much less of a sense of looking down from above onto what is essentially a map-like representation of the world. *Thomas the Clown* offers five interactive activities, which themselves differ from being simple sequencing tasks (Funny Faces and Building Blocks) through route finding (Ice Cream Break and Thomas the Postman) to programming a robot in a very similar way to working with Pixie (Strawberry Garden). Each activity has a number of skill levels. While this is more stimulating, perhaps, to children's imaginations, these activities do, of course, also suffer from being rather pre-set and rigid.

Conclusion

As with other areas of ICT, the technological possibilities and applications of control technology in the adult world are constantly changing and developing. The applications and simulations to which we introduce children are also changing, and their adult versions will be obsolete long before the children themselves finish their schooling. What we have attempted to demonstrate in this chapter, however, is that there are some underlying principles to which it is valuable to introduce young children. Through control technology activities, furthermore, it appears at least possible that young children are developing dispositions of mind and cognitive skills which will be of benefit to them as learners generally and beyond the realms of technology itself. From an ICT perspective, however, what is crucially important is that young children develop a confidence and an understanding about the fundamentals of this increasingly important area of technology, in order that they develop into technologically literate individuals. As in so many other areas, the early years educator can make a vital contribution in this one.

5

Interactive stories, simulated environments and adventure games

As we have noted earlier in Chapter 2, the most overwhelmingly common use of computers in the home for young children is currently to play games. In a small survey conducted by one of the present authors with the Reception and Year 1 classes in one small village primary school, over 20 different games played on home computers were mentioned by the children and their parents, many of them based on current Disney films or popular TV programmes (*Lion King, Bob the Builder, Tweenies* etc.). This games software comprises a variety of forms which might be usefully characterized as interactive stories, simulated environments and adventure games. At the same time as there is wide and increasing domestic use, there is relatively little use of such games in early years educational settings. The purpose of this chapter is to argue that there is considerable educational potential in computer-based game playing for young children with these kinds of software, which is currently not being exploited.

The chapter is in two parts. The first part attempts to define the essential characteristics of these kinds of computer-based games, and discusses the ways in which they usefully vary to provide progression and a range of different challenges. The second part explores the features of these kinds of games which make them ideally suited to helping children learn the skills of applying their knowledge and solving problems.

The essential characteristics of interactive stories, simulated environments and adventure games

In the last few years there has been a rapid expansion of software, mostly aimed at the domestic rather than the educational market, which has been designed for very young children. Much of this is in the form of interactive stories, simulated environments and adventure games. These programs all have game-like qualities which give them considerable educational potential, but they also vary in interesting ways that usefully give rise to possibilities for progression and skills development. In this section we want briefly to set out the range of programs currently available, and the educationally relevant ways in which they are the same and in which they vary. An understanding of these essential characteristics and modes of variation is important if we are to provide good quality games and a selection of games that offer a variety of opportunities within early years educational settings.

Essentially, we would suggest that the computer games currently available for young children have three educationally important characteristics and, in each of these, they also have important variations which offer opportunities for progression and development. First, and most importantly, they are all set within powerful story contexts to engage the interest and inspire the imaginations of young children. These contexts vary from the familiar and domestic to the fantastic and magical. Some programs present, for example, interactive versions of well-loved stories, such as Dorling Kindersley's *Three Little Pigs Interactive Storybook*, in which you can build a house out of bricks, help the pigs cross the river, and view the story from either the pigs' or the wolf's point of view. Another excellent example is Broderbund's *Just Grandma and Me* (from their delightful Living Books series), in which you can ride on a wind-blown umbrella, fend off a nasty crab or go snorkelling. Others depend upon and develop children's love of rhymes, such as Sherston's *Ridiculous Rhymes*, narrated by the ever-popular Tony Robinson, which capture wonderfully young children's love of the silly and the bizarre. *Albert's House* by Resource, *The Sherston Naughty Stories*, and the amazing *Catz, Dogz* and *Babyz* from Ubi Soft (Figure 5.1), on the other hand, are all examples set in familiar domestic situations. Other programs are set in the exciting fictional worlds of Fisher-Price's *Pirate Ship*, Infogrames' *Freddie Fish: The Case of* the *Hogfish Rustlers of Briny Gulch*, or Focus Multimedia's *Cosmic Family*, in which you meet Mr & Mrs Cosmic and family in their action-packed rocket.

The second and most important common feature of all of these programs is that, to varying degrees, they offer alternatives and the

Figure 5.1 *Babyz*

opportunity for children to choose and make decisions. In this sense they are intrinsically playful, and they put the child in control. They also stimulate thinking, discussion and trial and error learning. The variation here is enormous, as we noted in Chapter 3 when discussing this feature from the organizational point of view of offering children choices in a constrained and manageable way. In some of the simplest programs there is very much a fixed 'route' through the adventure or story. Even in simple interactive stories, however, each screen usually contains a number of 'buttons' or hot spots which produce an animated effect when the child clicks on them, or even just passes the cursor over them. Tivola's marvellous *Snow White and the Seven Hansels* shows, however, what can be done even with the interactive story format. Here, the child chooses which fairy tale to begin, but can then develop the story in all kinds of entertaining and novel ways, by muddling up the story developments. So when Little Red Riding Hood meets the seven dwarfs she has a dreadful time having to sew them all little red hoods (see Figure 5.2) just like her own and she comes to a sticky end also when she gnaws at the Gingerbread House and it collapses on top of her.

In many games now available, however, children are free to explore the environment in whichever way they wish. Whether the environment is a house, a pirate ship, a western town or a castle, children can decide to go wherever they like, play whichever game they like, and even, in for example the *Catz*, *Dogz* and *Babyz* series, rearrange the environment by moving items in it around. A further very exciting feature of some of these 'free environment' games is that the principal characters can be changed.

Figure 5.2   Little Red Riding Hood meets the seven dwarfs

In *Babyz*, for example, with the use of a microphone, you can teach your baby to talk and it will learn the words that you teach it. This explicit modelling of learning itself seems to us to be a potentially very significant development, as we discussed in more detail with regard to 'relational toys' in the earlier chapter on control technology.

Third, the games all vividly illustrate to children in very direct ways the nature of cause and effect. Their decisions and choices have consequences. This might be at the very simple level of clicking on a hot spot and watching the resulting animation. In Brilliant Computing's *Microworlds 2000*, for example, you can have hours of fun making the people in the house go to the toilet, make their lunch or watch the TV. As games become more sophisticated, however, the chains of cause and effect lengthen, and the child is required to become ever more strategic and planful. This is, of course, at the very heart of problem solving. This may be at the level of being required to find items around the different parts of the environment; so, in *Pirate Ship* (see Figure 5.3) you have to collect parts of the treasure map, and in Educational Insights' *Max and the Secret Formula* you are collecting the missing numbers from the formula. Even more sophisticated games, such as the classic *Granny's Garden* from 4Mation and *Lemmings* from Psygnosis, require you to construct increasingly complex series of moves to achieve your goal. By a process of trial and error you discover that you must go to the cupboard and get the broom so that you will have something to throw at the snake on the stairs in the witch's house, or that you must change one lemming into a blocker

Figure 5.3   Finding pieces of treasure map in *Pirate Ship*

to stop all the others walking off the precipice of a chasm while you change another into a builder to construct a bridge.

These gradual developments in early years games software towards giving the children more control and more choices, and requiring them to be gradually more planful, allow a very supporting and constructive progression to be present in the games to which we introduce them. The range of contexts should help us to ensure that all the children in our class or setting find games which are appealing, whether they prefer domestic drama or something more fantastic.

How adventure games help learning

It will be clear from the previous analysis that many of the computer games now available offer rich possibilities for entertaining young children. What we want to argue in this section, however, is that there is also ample evidence, from developmental psychology and class-room studies of children working at computers, to suggest that there are many features of computer games that make them ideally suited to helping children learn the skills of applying their knowledge and solving problems, thus:

- they encourage a playful approach to learning;
- they place problems in 'meaningful' contexts;
- they lend themselves to collaborative work and discussion;

- they involve children in many of the significant skills and processes involved in solving problems.

We want briefly to review each of these elements in turn. Together they give computer simulations and games the potential to help children learn in powerful and important ways.

The role of play in learning

As we discussed in Chapter 2, it would be easy to dismiss computer games on the grounds that they merely engage children in play. What is now well established among developmental psychologists and well understood by teachers of young children, however, is that play is one of the most powerful and effective mediums for children's learning. Many psychologists and educators have studied children's play, but perhaps some of the most influential and important work has been carried out by Jerome Bruner, who has argued that play is fundamental to human learning (see Bruner *et al.* 1976). Humans are distinguished from other species by their unique ability to think flexibly and to devise new ways to solve new problems. As we have reviewed earlier, Bruner has argued that our long period of biological immaturity, when we are being cared for by our parents, enables us to play far more and for much longer than any other species, and it is through play that we learn to be flexible and innovative in our thinking, and to become effective problem solvers. Play is an opportunity to try out different possibilities, to combine elements of a problem or situation in novel ways, to see what would happen if . . . all in complete safety.

Bruner's and other research has demonstrated that, for children and for adults, initially being given open-ended, exploratory and 'playful' tasks enhances problem-solving capability far more effectively than being introduced to a new area with carefully broken down, 'closed' tasks where the object at each stage is to produce the 'correct' answer. The relevance of computer games in providing playful opportunities for trying out different possibilities and developing flexible thinking is clear.

Other research has concerned different kinds of play (see Moyles (1989) for a review of work in this area). Within the literature a distinction has often been drawn between unstructured and structured play. In unstructured play children simply play in any way they like with the materials available. In structured play, often through some kind of adult intervention, children are posed problems, exposed to new possibilities, and so on. Overall, the evidence is that unstructured play is particularly valuable in enhancing emotional and social development, while structured play enhances intellectual development. Inasmuch as computer games are examples of relatively structured play, this is further confirmation that they are likely to be useful in fostering intellectual growth.

The importance of meaningful contexts

The study of the development of children's problem solving really began with the work of Jean Piaget. He argued that children pass through different stages of development. At each stage there are a different set of problems (such as his famous 'conservation' problems) which they are capable of solving because they have acquired a more sophisticated set of logical operations, or understandings. (See Wood (1998) for a review of Piaget's work.)

This basic position that children become better problem solvers because they become more logical has, however, as Wood (1998) argues, been seriously questioned by subsequent research. The problems young children have with Piaget's experiments appear to be more to do with their abstractness, or what has been called their 'disembeddedness'. As a consequence of their lack of experience, children are particularly dependent upon the context within which a task is placed. Where they are presented with a task which bears no relation to anything they already know and understand, they have great difficulty in making sense of it and of seeing which aspects of the task are relevant and which irrelevant to the problem posed. However, when tasks are placed in contexts which are meaningful to children, they are often able to demonstrate reasoning powers very similar to those evidenced by adults.

This recognition of the overwhelming significance of meaningful contexts for children's understandings and performance has led to new approaches to teaching in a number of curriculum areas. For example, the recent moves to engage children more with 'real books' as part of their early reading diet, the 'emergent writing' approach to children's early literacy development, and the recognition that children need to write for a variety of real purposes are all born of a recognition that children learn more effectively if the tasks they are set are meaningful from the child's perspective (see Hall 1989). Similar moves towards the use of real problems in mathematics are also beginning to take hold (see Atkinson 1992).

The advantages of the computer game kind of approach to problem solving flow just as directly from this aspect of children's performance. Rather than being faced with arid and obviously artificial problems of the 'if two men can dig a hole in three days' variety, children playing computer games become involved in a compelling story with characters with which they can identify and empathize, sometimes with goodies and baddies, with crises and setbacks and triumphs and, eventually, a satisfyingly happy ending. The children are involved in the story or adventure because they alone can help the king and queen find their lost children, or they have their very own baby to care for, or their curiosity has been aroused to find out what excitement will be in the next room. Such fictional contexts imbue the problems contained within them with real human motivations and purposes. This helps children understand the nature and meaning of problems, and thus enables them to maximize the use of their reasoning powers and learn from the experience most effectively.

The meaningful contexts provided by computer games also, of course, help to make them highly motivating. One of the present author's own first experiences of using an adventure game was with a class of 6-year-olds using *Granny's Garden* when it first came out as a program for the BBC almost 15 years ago. Some of the suggestions in the *Teacher's Handbook* were followed and the children developed some of their own, but what was so notable was the enthusiasm of their response. Children in this age group are, of course, very excited about fairy stories with witches and dragons and elves, and the program tapped into this area of interest very effectively (see Figure 5.4). But it was the problem-solving element of the program that really seemed to enthral them. The whoops of glee when each of the lost children was discovered were electric. If all the tasks we set children in school always elicited the level of involvement and perseverance that is consistently seen with interactive stories, simulations and adventure games then we would have long ago said goodbye to any problems of discipline, motivation, disruption, truancy and boredom.

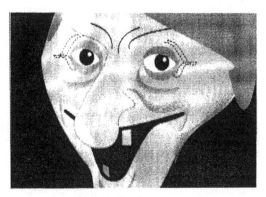

Figure 5.4   The witch from *Granny's Garden*

The value of collaborative problem solving

Recent research concerned with children's learning has also emphasized the significance of social interaction, either between adults and children, or between groups of children. This research derives from the writings of the Russian psychologist, Lev Vygotsky, and has been influenced also by the work of Jerome Bruner related to the role of language in learning (see Wood (1998) for a review). Two key aspects of the way in which language helps learning in the context of social interaction have emerged. First, it is clear that we come to understand ideas better through the process of articulating them in social or group problem-solving situations. Second, language is used in social contexts to 'scaffold', support and guide problem-solving processes and procedures. This kind of research has been partly responsible for a resurgence of interest during the last few years in the use of collaborative groupwork in primary classrooms (see Dunne and Bennett 1990).

In this context, it is interesting to note that, although initially thought of in terms of individualized learning, computers have generally been used by groups in classrooms, and the view of many teachers is that learning to work in groups is one of the main advantages of computer use in schools (Jackson *et al.* 1986). Crook (1994) has reviewed the extensive range of work now being carried out in schools involving collaborative learning with computers.

The effectiveness of groupwork in terms of children's learning, however, is dependent upon the quality of the talk and interactions generated. In relation to work with computers, recent evidence suggests that, not surprisingly, the pattern and quality of interaction between children is dependent upon the kind of software used. Significantly, the richest discussion has been found to be promoted by adventure games (Crook 1987).

Alongside this, there is now quite a range of research showing that children's development of effective problem-solving strategies is enhanced by working in pairs or small groups on computer-based tasks (Blaye *et al.* 1991). One of the present authors' own experiences with *Granny's Garden* and many other games would support this view that working in collaborative groups on these games provides a powerful environment for helping children to develop their problem-solving skills. The use of language to clarify ideas and understandings, and to support and guide problem-solving processes, has been very evident. *Granny's Garden* stimulated an enormous amount of talk and discussion among the class of 6-year-olds referred to above. This enabled them to persevere at, and solve the various puzzles much more effectively than they could have managed as individuals. They reminded one another about important information, provided a more varied selection of ideas and strategies and constantly checked one another's reasoning. They also shared out the work that needed doing, making it possible to manage the task in a way which any one of them would have found too demanding. Thus, while one read the on-screen instructions, another manipulated the keyboard and a third made written notes of important information (e.g. discovered passwords, listed helpful animals). The impact on the children's team-work and communicative skills in the few short weeks of this project was stunning.

Developing problem-solving skills and processes

Problem solving is a complex intellectual process involving the co-ordination of a range of demanding and interrelated skills. These skills include:

- understanding and representing the problem (including identifying what kinds of information are relevant to its solution);
- gathering and organizing relevant information;
- constructing and managing a plan of action, or a strategy;
- using various problem-solving tools;
- reasoning, hypothesis testing and decision making.

In a previous review of adventure games and simulations during the primary school phase, one of the present authors provided an extensive analysis of these slightly more sophisticated games in relation to these problem-solving elements (Whitebread 1997). Clearly, the simpler games which are appropriate for this younger age group do not develop these elements so extensively, but they are still there, as we explore below.

Understanding and representing the problem

A number of researchers have established that the way in which a problem is understood and mentally 'represented' has a major effect on the likelihood of it being solved. Children and adults who are better problem solvers have been found to spend longer encoding and repre-senting the problem to themselves before they start out on a solution. Within mathematics, for example, children commonly have difficulty recognizing which computational procedure they are required to do to solve word problems – this is known as the 'Is it an add, Miss?' syndrome, and will be recognized by all teachers of primary-aged children. This is linked to a second area of development, which is the ability to use existing knowledge. Children's abilities to solve problems can be significantly enhanced if they are simply required to review what they already know which might be relevant to the new task. This is particularly the case where children are being asked to transfer what they know to a new context or use what they know in a slightly different way.

Computer games are helpful here in at least two major ways. First, the fact that the problems are embedded in 'meaningful' contexts, as we have discussed, helps children enormously, and particularly helps them to see what is relevant and what is irrelevant.

Second, computer games can serve as excellent examples of the same kinds of problems arising in apparently very different contexts, which is vitally useful in helping children to learn to transfer ideas and processes. As a consequence, a progression of developing similar problem-solving skills but in different contexts can be achieved by using different games with the same underlying structure. This is relatively easy to achieve because there are a number of basic structures common to many simulations and adventure games. For example, there are several at different levels of difficulty which are essentially sequencing problems placed in the context of a search. You are searching for an object, or a set of objects, in an environment consisting of different rooms or locations. Some of the very simplest games aimed at children in the Early Years of Key Stage 1 are constructed in this way (e.g. *Darryl the Dragon*, *Max and the Secret Formula*, *Albert's House* and *Pirate Ship* all contain this element). The opening problem in *Granny's Garden* is also a good example. You must enter the woodcutter's house and find the first lost child. In order to do this you must go into the rooms in the correct sequence and make the correct decisions about whether to take the apple, what to throw at the snake, and so on. If you get the sequence wrong the witch catches you and you go back to the beginning again (and again and again!).

All these games share certain common features, and involve common problem-solving skills, but are couched in visually and imaginatively very different environments. Giving children the experience of applying skills and ideas they have learnt in one context to a new context which is superficially very different is enormously beneficial in helping them to learn how to tackle new problems. They learn to look for analogous problems they have encountered before, or things they know about which might be relevant. They also learn to analyse problems in terms of their underlying structure rather than their superficial characteristics. All this is highly significant in helping children to understand and represent new problems effectively.

Gathering and organizing information

Very much part of understanding the nature of a problem is recognizing what information is relevant to its solution. The essence of many real world problems is a lack of information. Children need to develop the skills of gathering relevant information and of organizing it in ways which will help them solve problems.

Once again, this is a central feature of many games. At its simplest, this may consist of being presented with particular pieces of information quite explicitly and being told you need to remember this. For example, it might be a password to get you on to the next stage of the adventure, as in *Granny's Garden*. Or it may be a matter of remembering the choice you made when you were last at this point in the forest, and Red Riding Hood finished up having a not very happy time with the Seven Dwarfs.

Simulations are particularly powerful in relation to this issue of gathering and organizing information. Good examples of this are Resource's *Albert's House* and *Number 62, Honeypot Lane*. In the former, information you have collected playing the simpler games involving just looking around the house becomes vitally important when you play the game where you have to help the mouse get back home past the cat. *Number 62, Honeypot Lane* is a more demanding program, probably more appropriate for children during Key Stage 1, which presents data on the events in a house over a calendar year by enabling you to set the date and time and then explore the house (see Figure 5.5).

In this program, there is total freedom in terms of the order in which the user views and collects information. In terms of children learning to

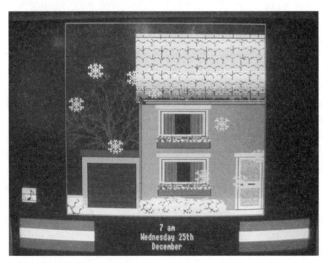

Figure 5.5 *Number 62, Honeypot Lane*

distinguish relevant and irrelevant information in relation to any particular problem, and of devising strategies for collecting relevant information, it therefore has real value. A huge variety of different problems can be devised, for example, in relation to the events at Number 62, Honeypot Lane, and different problems will require different search strategies for relevant information. Just to take one event, which is the arrival of the new baby, a whole range of different kinds of questions might be posed, thus:

- What special event takes place on 3 February? Find out as much as you can about this event.
- What begins to happen at one end of the bedroom on 21 January? Why does this happen?
- What is the baby's typical daily routine in July, and how is it different in October? Why do you think it changes?
- Where does the baby sleep in the afternoon, and for how long? Does the baby always sleep in the same place in the afternoons?

To answer some of these questions you have to start at a particular date and search the whole house. For others, you can start in a particular room. Some require you to go through the whole day, while for others you can concentrate on particular times. Some answers require only a limited number of pieces of information to be collected, while much more is needed for others.

Being able to recognize what information you need to solve a problem thus becomes of central significance when working with this kind of more open simulation, and gives this kind of program a particular value.

Planning and strategies
Being aware of the kind of information needed to solve a problem is also fundamental to being able to construct a plan of action. The ability to plan ahead is one of the great achievements of the human intellectual system. It is a highly complex skill relying largely upon our ability to form mental representations or models.

Children's planning abilities develop in two ways. First, they become able to construct and carry out plans which contain longer strings of 'moves' or elements. Second, their plans become more complex in structure, progressively containing subgoals, subroutines and strategies developed in other contexts and applied to the new problem. For example, it is sometimes necessary to take an action which appears to be moving you further away from the problem goal or solution, but is actually necessary to set up a situation from which you can proceed to a final solution. The classic problem of getting a dog, a cat and a mouse over a river using a boat that will only hold two of them at once is a case in point. The key move, which young children find very difficult, is to bring the cat back across the river to the starting point.

Being able to construct and use plans of action is a fundamental life skill. At the simplest level the organization of our daily lives depends upon it. Being a parent or a primary school teacher (or both!) necessitates a very high level of skilful planning. In commerce, science or industry it is equally vital. Even artists plan their painting, their concerto or their sculpture.

The fundamental skills of constructing plans and devising strategies can be very effectively practised through adventure games. We have already discussed above the common structure of many games which essentially involve discovering a successful sequence of moves through an environment which will reveal the necessary information and objects in the right order to allow problem solution. This is pure planning.

Another type of program which I would want to include under the heading of 'adventure games' also presents planning and strategy challenges of a particularly acute and motivating kind. This is the type of program where a sequence of moves has to be constructed and carried out under time pressure. Perhaps the pre-eminent example suitable for young children is the excellent *Lemmings* (early levels certainly manageable by 5- and 6-year-olds and the higher levels present a good challenge to 15-year-olds, but are obviously too difficult for most adults!). This kind of program is sometimes dismissed as just an 'arcade' game, but it could not be more different from the relatively mindless 'splat the aliens' type of program usually implied by this term. In *Lemmings*, each level sets the user a new challenge, and each new challenge is a mini-adventure in itself.

The basic problem scenario in *Lemmings* is that you have to get a certain proportion of a set of lemmings safely from one door where they enter the scene to another door where they leave (see Figure 5.6 for one of the simpler examples). From the moment you start the game lemmings keep coming through the entrance door and, although you can control the rate of their entrance to some extent, you have limited control of the speed at which they move and there is a time limit to solve the problem. At each level you are faced with a new scene through which the lemmings must travel. These scenes contain all kinds of obstacles and dangers. When a lemming hits an obstacle it simply turns round and walks back in the opposite direction. When it reaches a hole or a yawning chasm it simply walks off the end and plummets to its death.

To enable the lemmings to travel across the scene safely, you are able to transform any of them into different kinds of lemmings that perform

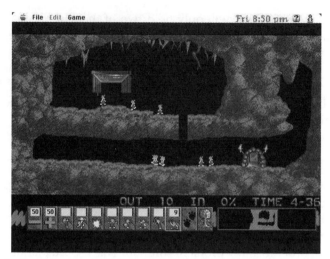

Figure 5.6   *Lemmings*: an early simple problem

certain tasks. These special lemmings can climb, dig holes, bash through obstacles, build bridges and even parachute. A lemming transformed into a 'blocker' becomes an obstacle and stops any more lemmings getting past that point. This can be a very useful strategy to give the climbers, diggers and builders time to construct a safe route before the rest of the lemmings get to that part of the scene. When all is prepared, sadly you then have to blow up the 'blocker', but his sacrifice is rewarded by all the other lemmings walking resolutely to safety through the exit door, and you are on to the next level!

Lemmings and other programs of similar design are a powerful agent in teaching children how to plan. At each level you can look at the problem scene before you start the lemmings and try to work out what to do. Once the lemmings start you try to put your first idea into action and the consequences are immediately obvious. The lemmings all plunge over the gap you have forgotten about, and so you work out how to deal with that. And so on until all the problems are solved and a safe route is devised. As the levels become increasingly harder you can use strategies devised at simpler levels to help solve part of the problem. There are all kinds of these strategies. I have mentioned the holding strategy using blockers. A strategy for long drops where there is solid ground at the bottom is to parachute a lemming down, turn him around (this might need you to parachute a second lemming down to become a 'blocker') and transform him into a builder to build a ladder back up, which the other lemmings can then walk down. This strategy is useful for the problem called 'A Ladder Might Be Handy' (see Figure 5.7).

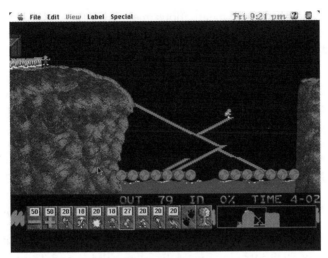

Figure 5.7 *Lemmings*: A Ladder Might Be Handy

It would not be such a useful strategy, however, for a long drop with water at the bottom. This will need a different strategy, probably involving digging down diagonally through the cliff, coming out near the bottom and then building a bridge from there. The range of possible combinations of the different kinds of lemmings means that many different strategies can be constructed, and many problems can be solved in a number of different ways.

What we see in all this is the opportunity for children to practise a number of key problem-solving skills. They are devising strategies which they then have to apply appropriately in different contexts and which they have to adapt and coordinate together in order to build a plan of action. The computer-based adventure game context is a powerful tool for learning these skills because it provides motivation and, to a probably unique extent, the opportunity for rapid trial and error learning.

Given careful planning and support by their educators, children can learn a great deal of importance by playing computer games. We cannot express the significance of this venture for children's education better than Loveless (1995):

> Our fast-changing, technological society requires individuals who can adopt this approach to learning through experience and investigation; who have a positive approach to problem solving, flexibility and transferability in new situations. 'Real' scientists, geographers, athletes, mathematicians, historians, artists, photographers, musicians and mountain climbers are able to be in

control and participate in situations, make hypotheses about what is going on and test them, and explore new possibilities in order to extend their understanding of the new and unpredictable.

(Loveless 1995: 71–2)

If we can help children to be in control of their learning and to deal more confidently and effectively with the unpredictable world they are entering, then we have performed a valuable service. Involving children in the engaging world of interactivie stories, simulations and adventure games can, we believe, make an important contribution to developing positive attitudes to problem solving and the vital skills needed to carry it out.

The important role of creative and problem-solving approaches across the early years and primary curriculum has been widely recognized and accepted by educators for many years (Fisher 1987; de Boo 1999; Craft 2000). The explicit introduction of 'Problem-solving and Thinking Skills' as cross-curricular skills into the latest version of the Primary National Curriculum (QCA 1999) was an important official recognition of this concern. The issue is not only about effective learning, however; it is also about children's enjoyment of learning and their feelings of self-efficacy and confidence in themselves as learners. This has now been officially recognized in the QCA's *Curriculum Guidance for the Foundation Stage* (QCA/DfEE 2000), which extends beyond 'Creative Development' and its associated 'Early Learning Goal', to include problem solving listed as an essential element within the 'Personal, Social and Emotional Development' area of learning:

Allowing children to think about and practise ways of solving problems helps them to gain confidence in themselves as problem-solvers, to develop the problem-solving habit and to feel capable of responding to self-chosen challenges.

(QCA/DfEE 2000: 29)

Using various problem-solving tools

One of the main reasons why adults can solve problems which are difficult for children is that we learn to use a range of problem-solving tools or 'heuristics' (Siraj-Blatchford and MacLeod-Brudenell 2000). Essentially, these consist of ways of recording information or constructing plans that can be applied to support our thinking when problems become too complicated and difficult for us to manage just in our heads. In the early years children often benefit from adults providing these heuristics to support or 'scaffold' their problem solving. Apart from breaking problems down into a sequence of stages, and directing the child's attention to specific aspects of a problem, appropriate heuristics often involve providing or encouraging the child to produce his or her own diagrams, measurements, maps, or models. In fact research suggests that mental visualization has a direct influence upon problem solving more generally (Antoniety 1991). Many adventure games use maps. Among those suitable for young children, *Granny's Garden*, for example, has a map in its final part. *Pirate Ship* has a see-through plan of the ship as its Activities Menu and a treasure map, of which you have to find the pieces. *Albert's House*, on the other hand, which involves the exploration of an environment, does not offer a map as such within the program, but this could usefully be provided. Quite a useful progression is to give children the experience of using a program with a map, and then helping them to construct their own map of an environment for which one is not provided. The drawing of 'my baby' or 'my favourite pirate', or the construction of models as an off-computer activity associated with particular games, is also clearly a useful exercise in getting young children to record information.

Reasoning, hypothesis testing and decision making
The human intellectual processing system doesn't just gather information. Constructing a plan, or deciding to use a particular strategy, is dependent upon a number of active and more fine-grain reasoning skills which enable us to integrate separate pieces of information into new knowledge. These skills include those of making inferences and deductions, generating and testing predictions or hypotheses, and of making decisions. Crucially, they are about applying what you already know to new situations.

As Loveless (1995) has pointed out, simulations and adventure games provide a wealth of opportunities for children to practise these vital reasoning skills. Different kinds of games provide opportunities for different kinds of reasoning. Opportunities are provided sometimes, for example, for the children to apply their real-world knowledge to a problem, such as when they are asked which option (e.g. an animal, or a tool) they wish to use to help them solve a particular problem. The kind of adventure game which is essentially concerned with constructing a sequence of moves involves the children in making predictions about what will happen next if a particular move is made. Thus, the children make hypotheses and then test them. The kind of game which is more concerned with exploring a simulated world provides different challenges. In *Number 62, Honeypot Lane* (Resource), for example, you only see static 'snapshots' of the various parts of the house on each hour and you never actually see most of the people living in the house (apart from the odd arm or back of a head).

Consequently, you have to make deductions about events largely from the changing location of objects. Thus, the baby's daily routine in its early months can be partly inferred from the location of the pram, which is in the hall when the baby is in the cot, outside in the garden when it contains the baby, and nowhere to be seen when the baby has gone shopping with Mum. The opportunities provided by this program for reasoning and discussion are consequently enormous.

6

Creativity, communication and the computer

Creativity and problem solving are often considered to be closely related and, given the foregoing arguments concerning the relevance of visual representation, it is perhaps surprising that the 'Creative Development' section of the *Curriculum Guidance for the Foundation Stage* (QCA/DfEE 2000) makes no reference to the use of a computer (although it does refer to the use of television and tape recorders). Paint and drawing programs are widely used in pre-schools and music programs such as Topologica's *Music Box* have also been shown to have a great deal of potential. Art and craft activities are important in the early years because they provide opportunities for children to express themselves with colours, shapes and textures, and to develop their fine muscle control at the same time. A wide range of materials are commonly available in nurseries such as paint, plasticine, crayons, and play dough. As the children draw, paint and make things, they are making choices, trying things out, exploring, experimenting and solving problems (Siraj-Blatchford and MacLeod-Brudenell 2000). Computer programs cannot replace these experiences, but they can add to them if they are used wisely.

Using a paint program, the child learns to control the mouse which acts as an extension of her hand in a similar way to a crayon or paint brush. But the visual feedback on the screen is indirect and as the child is unable to see both her hand and the screen at the same time, this makes coordination especially difficult. Figure 6.1 shows some of the alternatives available. The use of digital graphics tablets are therefore more appropriate for drawing and painting in the early years. A typical 'tablet' provides a

| Mini mouse | Track ball | Graphics tablet | Touch screen |

Figure 6.1   Alternatives to the standard mouse

digital pencil or stylus for computer drawing and painting. With the use of drawing and painting software, techniques can be tried out and practised, and mistakes are easily corrected. The use of these tools may therefore empower children to achieve much more than they would otherwise be capable of. Even watercolour and oil painting can be simulated on some programs.

Where a mouse is used for these purposes care should be taken to ensure that it is small enough for the child to hold. There are many kinds of mice on the market and there are also track balls, and track pads available for young children. Some nurseries are also using computers with touch-sensitive screens to good effect. Touch screens have been used to provide for special educational needs for many years.

Using a program such as *Dazzle*, the educator can control the number of tools available on the toolbars. The software provides a means by which the adult may provide appropriate levels of challenge for a range of individuals and groups.

While Margie Jones and Min Liu (1997) found the keyboard to be the most appropriate input device for 2- to 3-year-olds, touch screens allow children to use their fingers to point directly to objects on the screen. Sensitive transparent panels are available that may be clipped onto a standard computer screen but (at the current time) a purpose-built 14″ touch monitor that costs about £500 may be found easier to set up, and, as Littler (1999) has suggested, they are practically indestructible. Touch screens are ideal for special needs pupils and for use in nurseries where the children find other kinds of data entry devices difficult to use. Touch screens provide a means by which children may be empowered to use more sophisticated software applications than are otherwise access-ible without the distraction of having to position a track ball or mouse or find particular keys. Switches are also available to provide a simple means of interaction (see Granada Learning in Appendix B).

In discussing the limitations of drawing with a mouse, Beeching (2002) argues that it is a case of the 'tail wagging the dog' where the technology actually serves to inhibit the 'natural' process of drawing: 'Whether using pencils, pens, or brushes, that requires a sensitivity and control completely foreign to the computer mouse and drawing tablet' (Beeching 2002). Beeching, a former NBC art director, equates drawing with a computer mouse with drawing by looking into a mirror. As he says, when drawing with a mouse children have no direct contact with the materials, and their work rarely contributes very much towards the development of visual awareness. The 'forgiving' nature of the 'undo' facility, and the provision of extensive (prescribed) colour palettes are also seductive:

> The most insidious element of the insensitive mouse is its propensity toward false ease of use. Once activated, a child can scribble with the mouse to his or her heart's content without once questioning the quality of the shape and form.
>
> (Beeching 2002)

Beeching's major argument is that, while technology can be beneficially applied to liberate us from repetitive tasks, it shouldn't be applied to downgrade human experience. Graphic artists use computers to save time in producing page layouts, paste-ups, and typesetting. But computers are seen to have little to offer when it comes to line drawing! Even more importantly:

> When children are exposed to the legitimate processes and skills of drawing and painting, they will be in better positions to recognize the difference between computer-generated imagery and the real thing.
>
> (Beeching 2000)

So what are the implications for using painting and drawing software with young children? If we have a scanner, and this is now a relatively inexpensive computer peripheral, we should make the most of what painting and drawing software is designed for. As Linderoth (2000) has suggested, we should encourage the children to produce their line drawings on paper with a pencil or felt pen and then scan their image into the computer. The 'paint bucket' or 'fill' facilities within the program can then be used to save the child the tedium of 'colouring in'. Scanning the picture also offers the possibility of copying the image to make multiple pictures for Christmas or other greeting cards, invitations etc. The digital image might also be communicated to parents or other relatives at home or at their workplace as email attachments, or 'posted' in the children's art gallery featured on the pre-school website (see http://www.ioe.ac.uk/cdl/datec for some good examples).

In Reggio Emilia nurseries of northern Italy, young children have been shown to be very capable when it comes to representing their ideas. The Reggio Emilia approach is based upon parental involvement, the development of aesthetically pleasing environments, and collaboration toward common goals. As Edwards and Springate (1995) have argued, we need to recognize that exploration, representation, and communication feed one another, and a great deal can be achieved when we work with children towards these combined ends. The documentation of young children's work provided by Reggio Emilia educators highlights young children's amazing capabilities and indicates that it is through the unity of thinking and feeling that young children can explore their world, represent their ideas, and communicate with others at their highest level. According to Edwards and Hiler (1993), there are four principles that we should take from Reggio Emelia that may be applied whenever we plan art and creative activities:

1 Young children are already developmentally capable of high-level thinking skills, including *analysis* (e.g. seeing similarities and differences); *synthesis* (e.g. rearranging, reorganizing); and *evaluation* (judging the value of materials). We should encourage them to practise these skills.

2 Young children express their ideas in a variety of ways using a variety of symbolic media. When we encourage them to share their experiences and learn from others they can develop their expressive repertoire even further.

3 Young children benefit from open-ended discussions, and meaningful long-term 'topic' or investigation-based activities. Curriculum integration really works in the early years, and language, science, design and technology, social studies, dramatic play, and artistic creation may all be usefully brought together to create meaningful activities that are relevant to the child's life experiences.

4 Young children especially benefit from open-ended projects which are started either from a chance event, a problem posed by one or more children, or an experience planned and led in a flexible way by teachers. The adult role in these activities is to provide material and intellectual support and guidance, and to act as partners to the children in the process of discovery and investigation: 'They take their cues from children through careful listening and observation, and know when to encourage risk-taking and when to refrain from interfering.'

Edwards and Springate (1995) provide further guidance on the role of adults in arguing that

Children's best and most exciting work involves an intense or arousing encounter between themselves and their inner or outer world. Teachers provide the occasions for these adventures. Children find it hard to be creative without any concrete inspiration. Instead, they prefer to draw on the direct evidence of their senses or memories. These memories can become more vivid and accessible through the teacher's provocations and preparations. For example, teachers can encourage children to represent their knowledge and ideas before and after they have watched an absorbing show, taken a field trip, or observed and discussed an interesting plant or animal brought into class. Teachers can put up a mirror or photos of the children in the art area, so children can study their faces as they draw their self-portrait. Teachers can offer children the opportunity to check what they have drawn against an original model and then let them revise and improve upon their first representation.

Edwards and Springate (1995) refer to a number of activities that might usefully be developed using digital images, although the images of young children that they suggest might be cut and pasted into scrapbooks to support their learning about childhood might as easily be used in the production of Microsoft Powerpoint or screensaver presentations.

Manipulating digital images

Linderoth (2000) argues that in postmodern cultural contexts where images are routinely reappropriated, copied, edited and distributed for different purposes we should provide children with early and ongoing experience in the manipulation of images in order to support their emergent critical graphic awareness and media literacy:

> To become aware of the role of technology in culture is a central part of developing computer literacy. This includes being aware of how technology has totally changed the conditions under which images are produced and distributed.
>
> (Linderoth 2000)

Linderoth argues that it is crucial for children to understand that the photographic image has lost its status of representing 'reality'. He goes on to argue that this awareness may be developed in the early years through encouraging children to edit pictures themselves. Children thus become aware of the conditions under which images are produced and may themselves produce images that are similar to those they see in cartoons, for example. These often feature large areas of a single colour which children sometimes attempt to emulate using paint or crayons with little success.

Figure 6.2   A monster

Yet with PhotoShop or some other tool for editing pictures, children can easily fill scanned line drawings, just like a professional cartoonist. Note: Linderoth's detailed instructions for carrying this out may be found on the first DATEC website (http://www.ioe.ac.uk/cdl/datec).

The picture of a monster in Figure 6.2 was inspired by Pókemon, and the technology allowed the child who created the image to 'try out' a number of different colours before she opted for the final version.

Software also provides a means by which images can be resized and reshaped in a variety of ways. Figure 6.3 provides a typical example of a 6-year-old's experimentation with this as she designed a Christmas card. Digital cameras may be used to document ongoing activities at the nursery. When these are presented, children gain an insight into other children's work and teachers have the opportunity to give feedback on the children's accomplishments. As Linderoth (2000) argues, the images may also provide a natural focus for parents leaving and picking up their children:

> The images provide teachers and parents with some material to talk about. Parents get some insights into what their children have done during the day and teachers can more easily communicate to parents what activities, aims, themes etc. they are working with at the moment.

Digital media may also be employed to provide opportunities for children to tell stories in a narrative form. While multimedia authoring packages like *My World* (Granada Learning), *Kid Pix*, *Junior Multimedia* (Sherston) or *Hyperstudio* may be beyond the capabilities of the children working on their own, many nurseries have shown that a great deal can be achieved with adult support. A good example of this is provided by a program called *Elmo's World* (Mattel Media). In *Elmo's World*, children are encouraged to outline and then colour pictures of animals which are then animated by

Figure 6.3   Chelsea's image manipulation

Figure 6.4   *Elmo's World*

the software. It is an excellent concept, and with adult support it can be very rewarding. Figure 6.4 shows Elmo driving the animated train.

Again, a major bonus here is to be achieved in introducing children at an early age to the methods by which significant features of their world (e.g. cartoons) are made. Such activities provide support for the development of technological literacy. Much of this kind of work requires the children's use of equipment such as digital cameras and scanners, and if they are to understand the operation of these devices then careful choices need to be made to ensure that their operation is as transparent and intuitive as possible. Unfortunately, at the present time many digital cameras and scanners are far from ideal in this respect. Reference was made in Chapter 1 to the Sony Mavica digital camera that saves images onto a floppy disk. When the child (or adult) has taken a photograph, at first they see the image on the LCD screen; they can then remove the disk (with the photo on it) from the camera and when they put it into the computer, a double-click brings the picture directly onto the computer screen. At the time of going to press a scanner that provides for the transfer of an image directly to the screen in a one touch (switch) operation is manufactured by Hewlett Packard. Other similar products may soon be available.

Of course, one of the most liberating features of early childhood education is provided by the children's own relatively unfettered imaginations, and none of these technical problems are so significant when the ICT hardware that the children are using is 'only [sic] pretend'!

The internet and world wide web

The internet provides a significant source of multimedia resources and no discussion of the subject would be complete without making reference to this advanced application of ICT. The world wide web (www) is made up of many millions of computers connected across the world, all serving up their own 'web pages'. While most personal computer users limit their activity to simply accessing or downloading other people's pages, anyone with their equipment connected up correctly can become a part of this web. DfES (2002) statistics showed that already 96 per cent of schools reported that they were connected to the internet compared to 86 per cent in 2000. While there is every indication that Scottish pre-schools may be taking the lead, pre-schools across the UK will undoubtedly catch up fast. According to the Which (2002a) Internet Online Survey, as many as 19 million people in the UK are now using the internet although only 46 per cent of them are women. Almost 8 million people in the UK have shopped online so e-commerce is clearly beginning to make an impact. For most users, to access the internet their PC must be equipped with a modem that allows it to connect up to an internet service provider (ISP) via a telephone line. There are currently more than a hundred ISPs to choose from in the UK, with the bigger companies usually offering the most reliable service with fewer breakdowns. One of the most basic affordances offered by internet access is email and the statistics show that in each of the preceding two years the percentage of teachers and pupils who had personal email accounts more than doubled.

Carter (2001) reported on how a child being away from her Reception class for a few weeks following an accident provided the stimulous for developing an email project that was later implemented right across the school. As Carter reports, the project proved to be extremely enjoyable and worthwhile to the 4- and 5-year-olds:

> As the first messages began to arrive from parents, I took to checking the email with the children as part of first registration and during our regular 'Snack and Chat' session after first break.

Some typical messages were as follows:

```
Hello James and classmates
Did you all have a good lunch?
Have a fun afternoon
From Di, James's mum
```

```
Hi Mum
I'm having a lovely time. Its fun. There's a lot of
bricks. I got a sticker on my jumper from Mrs Palmer
because I did a picture of the whole city waking up.
Love from James
```

One child was especially thrilled when she received a reply from both her parents within half an hour:

```
Hello!
I was just playing in the home corner. I was the mummy.
Jenny was the five year one and Gavin was dressed up as the
policeman. It was good.
I've had a lovely day today
Hugs and kisses
Rosie
XXXXXXXXXX
```

```
Dear Rosie
Hello - its mummy here. I've got back to my desk and found
your letter. This is the nicest email I have had today
and I am very happy to hear from you!
I will see you later - remember I will pick you up from
Mandy's house
Love Mummy
```

```
Rosie
Nice to hear you've been having fun on the computer
Daddy
```

To make sure that every child felt a part of the activity the Reception teacher supported the children in sending emails to other staff or children within the school. All of the children were therefore involved in the project. Sometimes a child even emailed the class from home when they were not away unwell:

```
Hello every body.
When you read this it will be Friday 13th October and its
my Birthday! I am 5 years old.
I think I am the oldest in the Panda's class
Am I right?
From Gary
```

While most internet users access the world wide web via a personal computer (PC), *digital television* is seeing rapid growth in the UK and there are plans to make all of these cable, terrestrial broadcasting and satellite systems web-enabled. Several web browsers now offer speech including IBM's *Home Page Reader* (http://www.austin.ibm.com/sns/hpr). As Benjamin (2000) argues, there are now hundreds of children's websites on the internet and they are getting better and better. In fact it may be only a matter of time until the internet takes over as the major source of children's software (see early education sites listed in Appendix C).

The 'price' that we seem to have to pay for this amazing resource of applications, information and material is that the universal free access applies to everyone, even those who haven't a care about the welfare of children, and even those who wish to exploit them. It is technically possible for anyone to publish anything that they want to. Therefore, if children are to be protected from pornographic or other inappropriate material, then their access has to be limited, or offending websites have to be filtered out. While some educators and parents in Europe apparently feel that it is better to teach children about the dangers of the internet rather than to protect them from them (http://schoolsite.edex.net.uk/1475/report.htm), the majority in the UK believe that children should be protected. Pre-schools linked to a local education authority network are all protected through filtering. Others may take advantage of services provided by their internet service provider, e.g. America Online (AOL) which provides 'parental controls', or they may invest in blocking

Figure 6.5 'Grand Theft Auto'

software such as that provided by NetNanny or CyberPatrol. But it should be recognized that these filters rely on the company first identifying the offensive material so that it can be blocked and this isn't always 100 per cent successful. When Which© reviewed internet filters in May 2002, including that provided by the Content Rating Association (ICRA), they found them to be ineffective.

The best way around this is to create your own custom web portal, and products such as CyberDuck's KidsWeb and BrowserLock (http://www.BrowserLock.com) provide a means by which you can do just that. Children are then able to browse their internet unattended. Links to all websites outside the list that you have specified will be disallowed.

Adults should therefore closely supervise young children when they browse the www; they should also expain the dangers and stress the importance of not giving personal information to strangers. Children are vulnerable to advertisers, to pornography and to the portrayal of gratuitous violence.

Unfortunately it isn't just the internet that provides inappropriate content for young children, and violent or otherwise inappropriate video games sometimes get passed on between siblings or friendship groups. An especially well known example of this genre is provided by 'Grand Theft Auto' which allows the 'player' (among other things) to drive over pavements and run over pedestrians (Figure 6.5). Nurseries and pre-schools need to monitor the use of all new software and develop an awareness of the potential problems. For a good introduction to the issues see the UNESCO International Clearinghouse on Children and Violence on the Screen (http://www.nordicom.gu.se).

In the further development of policies, the criteria associated with sex and violence that are offered in the Advertising Standards Authority code of practice may be usefully applied to a range of contexts (including cartoons):

Particular diligence must be exercised in matters of violence and sexual violence . . . materials must not condone nor encourage anti-social behaviour of this kind. Nor should they play on the fears of the vulnerable. Depictions of and references to weaponry, especially those weapons which are easily obtainable in the UK and are potentially attractive to violent minds, should be avoided or presented with great care.

With these broad definitions in mind, there follows a list of specific areas which should be either avoided or treated with great caution. It should be emphasized that this list is not intended to be comprehensive and there may be other matters that could infringe generally accepted levels of taste and dignity:

- Sexual violence or threats
- Juxtaposition of violence and nudity
- Aggression towards vulnerable women or children
- Linking violence with children
- Direct threats to defenceless victims
- Torture
- Immediate threat of death
- Weapons pointed directly at viewer
- Realistic horror effects – gross violence, dismemberment, disintegration and death
- Excessive blood or gore – especially on weapons such as knives
- Sexual or violent images having no reference to the game
- Excessive weaponry
- Prosecutable weapons – chainsticks, crossbows, flick knives etc.
- Drug abuse
- Overt sexual activity
- Excessive tastless nudity
- Derogatory ethnic or racial images or text
- Text that promises brutality, torture, sexual violence or humiliation
(http://www.eispa.com/codeprac/asa.html)

7

Conclusions: The way forward

When we think of technologies in schools, it is important to be clear about whether we are talking about a long-term perspective – what is going to happen in twenty years or in ten years time – or are we thinking about what is going to happen tomorrow . . . We can only make small changes. But stop thinking of the small changes as making little improvements in the system as we know it. Think of the small changes as steps towards preparing for the big change to come. So we need a vision of where it is going, and then how to prepare.

(Papert 1998)

In Chapter 3 we suggested that you might find it useful to think back to the kinds of technologies being used by adults when you were a child. We asked you to consider how relevant an education based on developing skills to apply those technologies would have been for you. Our own educational experiences were particularly inappropriate in those terms. Many of the technologies that we were taught in school in the 1950s and 1960s (e.g. the wrought-iron metalwork and blacksmithing!) had already at that time been largely abandoned. For one of us there were opportunities to learn a little about electronics in after-school clubs and hobby groups. This led to further education in electronic thermionic 'valve' technology and consequent employment as an electronics engineer in industry. But when transistors were first introduced much of the knowledge and the skills that had been developed in working with valve circuits became redundant. Further education was needed to learn about the new technology, and many of the old skills became obsolete. Some years later the same thing happened again with the advent of integrated circuit 'chips'. But the deskilling at this stage was even more profound because the technology had become disposable, and there was no longer very much call for the in-depth knowledge and understanding of electronics required to trace faults at a component level. This was the point at which the decision was made to become a teacher.

It may be that schools and colleges today are more responsive to the social and economic needs of society but it is always difficult to predict the future forms that technology will take. In this book we have argued that if we seek to support children in their ICT education for the future then we should look to the underlying attitudes and skills that they may develop through interactions with the advanced technology that we have. But we should not be seduced into thinking that what they learn in the classroom today will be of too much direct relevance to their experiences in the future. If we are to speculate about the future of technology, it is wise to learn from the past. Many readers will recall the most popular classroom computer of the 1980s – the Acorn 'BBC B' (Fig. 7.1). Software for the 'BBC' could at first only be loaded from cassette tapes, and then later from 7" and then 3.5" diskettes and ROM chips. It was developed originally by a small development team at Acorn which included an influencial group of Cambridge University students, and more than a million of these computers were sold. The major features of the BBC were:

- a 2 MHz 6502 processor (which enabled it to do two million operations at a time);

Figure 7.1 BBC Computer

- a 32 KB random access memory (RAM) (that was 16 KB in the 'model A' and 64 KB in the later models).

One of the most significant computer developments came with the graphical user interface (GUI). Users will recall that the BBC computer didn't have a 'desktop' on which you could 'double click' or 'drag and drop' icons that represented different files and applications. To load a program, program commands had first to be entered at the blinking cursor on the screen.

We can thank Macintosh for the GUI which we now take for granted, and a typical PC available in the shops now sports as much as:

- 2 GHz Pentium processors (i.e. two billion operations at a time);
- 64 MB Ram as standard (with 500+ MB commonly available).

Modern computers also have CD ROM drives with capacities of 700MB, and DVD drives that can store up to 17 GBs (enough to store a two-hour movie with a soundtrack, interviews, games etc.). The cutting edge of ICT right now seems to have come with the convergence of mobile computing and communications technologies and with interactive television. Generation 3 (G3) mobile telephones are already on sale that allow users to browse the world wide web and transmit video pictures along with their voice messages. Research and development in the industry is largely focused upon portable and 'ubiquitous computing', computers built in to a wide variety of everyday artefacts and devices (including clothing). 'Ubiquitous computers' communicate with each other using the latest wireless and 'blue tooth' technologies to respond to and provide for individual needs.

Alan Kay of Apple has referred to this as *third paradigm* computing. In the first paradigm he argues that mainframe computers were shared by lots of people, then came the personal desktop computer, but in the new age of ubiquitous computing the idea is that the technology recedes into the background of our lives. Both Microsoft research, and the Massachusetts Institute of Technology (the MIT Project Oxygen) are currently working on a new generation of devices that provide for voice and visual interaction with the built environment. In fact it may not be very long at all before we are all speaking to the walls like John-Luke Picard does on the Starship *Enterprise*!

It would probably be a good idea if the educational technology was integrated into educational activities to the extent that it 'disappeared', so that it became unnoticed in just the same way as we no longer notice paper and pencil when it comes to writing. We simply take them for granted, and the new technology should probaby be the same.

But the hypertext structure of the www is also quite different from that of traditional means of communicating information through the printed word. Traditionally text was presented in a linear and sequential manner determined by its author or editor. But as Alexandersson and Pramling Samuelsson (1998) have argued, information is now presented without a set sequence, in a non-linear and associative way. Children are able to explore texts spontaneously and freely, going from one link to another, in any direction that they find interesting. There are no set tracks to be followed. Alexandersson and Pramling Samuelsson go on to argue that while children need to develop both linear and associative ways of thinking, the influence of hypertext reading might be that their thinking becomes more liberated and creative. Another possibility is that less linear thinking may influence their development of the ability to think in a logical and deductive way (Hundeide 1991). More research is clearly required in this and in many other ICT areas if we are to respond appropriately in education.

As previously suggested, many children are already using a range of sophisticated technologies and we still know very little about their learning impact. A wide range of relational toys have recently been introduced that include Furbies, Tamagotchis, and robotic puppies such as Techno and Aiebo. These toys present themselves as having 'affective' states and being capable of learning new language or movements from their interactions with children. According to Turkle (1998), such toys embody the construction of 'sort of alive'. A number of claims have also been made regarding the developmental potential of children playing with these toys. As we have argued, these include the idea that children will learn about learning (develop a metacognitive awareness) from playing with toys that learn. Toy designers clearly have an important role to play in providing the educational technologies of the future. But the key questions still to be addressed include: How do young children understand relational and robotic toys? What do children learn from their interactions with them? What influence do the toys have on children's development? What learning opportunities can be identified and realized in practice? We can only look to future research for answers to these questions.

According to the British Educational Communications and Technology Agency (BECTa) (2001), primary schools with better Information and Communications Technology (ICT) resources achieve better grades for their pupils in Key Stage 2 national tests for English, mathematics and science. But in the context of early childhood, computers have often been dismissed as being at best purely recreational and at worst positively harmful in the context of children's education and development.

However, we have argued that in the case of interactive stories, programmable toys, simulated environments, creativity, communication, and adventure games, the opposite is the case. We have also argued that technological literacy is a citizenship issue. Children have a right to a broad and balanced education. As the Education Reform Act of 1988 emphasizes, all schools should offer a broad and balanced curriculum that prepares children 'for the opportunities, responsibilities and experiences of adult life'. There can be no doubt that Information and Communications Technology will feature strongly in the adult lives of the young children we are working with today. All of the evidence we have from psychological studies of children's learning, and from research directly focused on children working at computers, is that these computer games and applications offer powerful opportunities for children's learning and for the development of their problem-solving and creative abilities.

When computers were first introduced into primary school classrooms in the early 1980s it was largely in the context of mathematics education and there was quite a degree of emphasis on games and puzzles. Over the period of the last decade, however, as computers have become a more established part of primary and early years provision, the focus within primary school ICT has shifted away from problem solving and games towards either computer uses which are paralleled in the adult world of work (word processing, managing databases etc.), or towards software which is attempting explicitly to 'teach' children to read, spell, count. The problem with this is that computers have been grafted on to the existing curriculum in support of existing priorities, rather than changing those priorities. While adventure games and simulations have been explicitly included in the National Curriculum framework, they have tended to be narrowly defined as an aspect of 'modelling', which has been until fairly recently a relatively neglected aspect of ICT within many classrooms and settings. A publication by the Schools Curriculum and Assessment Authority (SCAA 1995) does provide an illustration of modelling work with an adventure game at Key Stage 1, and there is some recognition of the role of such programs in supporting the development of children's speaking and listening skills. But as Papert (2001) has suggested, for school teachers to go very far in this direction might be like adding a jet engine to a stage coach: it couldn't be achieved without shaking the vehicle apart. Thankfully we are not in that situation in the pre-school sector.

In order for computer-based technology to make a serious educational contribution, it needs to be used by young children in ways which recognize how they learn most effectively, and in ways that help them to become confident and creative thinkers. In this context, we have argued that computer-based games of the kinds indicated have the potential to make a very powerful contribution.

Of course there are software programs that are inappropriate for use in early childhood and we have already referred to some of the general problems with the application of programmed learning software. It is difficult to see what positive learning might arise from application of some of the popular arcade games software as well. There are also programs available in the shops that feature excessive violence and other adult themes. Children sometimes have access to these programs at home and it is important that parents and pre-schools have thought through and adopted policies in this area. But apart from these general provisos, we believe there is often too much emphasis placed upon the age appropriateness of software. We have seen many occasions where pre-school children have gained a great deal from interactions with adults that have been focused around their collaborative use of adult software such as a word processor, and the use of digital cameras and Powerpoint. An appropriate evaluation of these products therefore needs to be made in terms of their application in an educational environment where adults and children play and learn together, and not simply upon children's ability to use them on their own.

In a recent DfES-sponsored exploration of the contribution that games can make to the education process, *Teachers Evaluating Educational Multimedia* (McFarlane *et al.* 2000) asked Foundation Stage and Key Stage 1 educators to evaluate a range of appropriate games, including 'edutainment' titles like Bob the Builder and Tweenies and adventure games in the Pajama Sam and Freddi Fish series. The educators reported that they found evidence of learning in all of the six areas of learning in the Foundation Stage Early Learning Goals, including:

Personal and social education
  I. Provide interest and motivation to learn
  II. Maintain attention and concentration levels
  III. Can work as part of a group and can learn to share resources

Language and literacy
  I. Encourage children to explain what is happening
  II. Sustain attentive listening, responding to what they have heard by relevant comments, questions or actions
  III. Use talk to organize, sequence, and clarify thinking, ideas, feelings and events

Mathematical development
  I. Use everyday words to describe position

Creative development
  I. Recognize and explore how sounds can be changed, sing simple songs from memory, recognize repeated sounds and sound patterns and match movements to music
  II. Respond in a variety of ways to what they see, hear, smell, touch and feel
  III. Use their imagination in art and design, music, dance, imaginative and role-play and stories

(McFarlane *et al.* 2000: 13–14)

Some of these educational experiences were clearly to be had while the children were working at the computer, and some were clearly richly imaginative and creative off-computer experiences stimulated by the games. The crucial question here is how those less experienced educators sort out what is appropriate from what is not. As TechKnowLogica (http://TechKnowLogica.org, Editorial, October 2001) have also argued, it is often difficult to discern the quality educational software from games and entertainment. It seems that as many as 678 new children's software titles were released in the year 2000 alone. In Chapter 1 we recommended the criteria developed in the DATEC project. TechKnow-Logica offer the following suggestions for evaluating what they call 'basic learning tools':

User friendliness – Can the supervising adult use it easily as a teaching tool? Can the child use it with minimum guidance so s/he can interact with the program without technological concerns?

Age appropriateness – Does the software contain intellectual content appropriate to the child's age cohort?

Appropriate content – Does the program contain violent, sexual or discriminatory content?

Clear learning goals – Are there clear learning goals for each exercise, game or lesson?

Reward success – Does the program incorporate fun ways to reward the child for success? Are explanations offered when children receive correct and incorrect answers?

Graphics – Does the program use graphics, music, video clips, web links and other multimedia material to supplement and enhance the child's opportunities to learn more about a subject?

Reviews – Has the software received positive reviews from reputable education or parenting websites or journals?

There are now quite a number of internet review sites (e.g. http://www.superkids.com and http://www.childrenandcomputers.com). But many reviews that will be found on the internet have been carried out by people who are untrained, or, even worse, by people who have an interest in marketing the product. One independent source of expert reviews in the UK is to be found at the new DATEC website: http://www-datec.educ.cam.ac.uk. Reliable software reviews relevant to National Curriculum Key Stage 1 are also to be found on http://TEEM.org

A recent WhichOnline (2002b) report on software in pre-schools credibly emphasized the importance of adult interaction (see Siraj-Blatchford and Siraj-Blatchford 2003), and they recommended *Jump Ahead 2000* and *Reader Rabbit Nursery*. But the WhichOnline review was focused on just seven products: *Reader Rabbit Toddler* (The Learning Company); *Reader Rabbit Thinking Adventures* (The Learning Company); *Jump Ahead 2000 Pre-School* (Havas); *My First CD-ROM: Toddler School* (Dorling Kindersley); *Learning Ladder: Pre-school* (Dorling Kindersley); *Winnie the Pooh Toddler* (Disney Interactive); and *Star Wars Learning Activity Centre* (Lucas Learning). The titles were selected simply on the basis of market criteria and, while the WhichOnline review involved both parent and 'expert' reviewers, it may be significant that the 'experts' favoured a different package to the two recommended by WhichOnline, because it encouraged parental interaction (*My First CD-Rom Toddler School*). They were also impressed with the 'real life' images that supplemented the animation in this software.

The WhichOnline experts felt that some of the *Reader Rabbit Nursery* applications were too challenging for younger children and that the navigation was 'not always straightforward'. When recommending software we should, of course, ask the children themselves what preferences they have. There is some evidence that children's ratings match those of the experts (Escobedo and Evans 1997), although it is debatable which group's evaluations are corroborated by this.

The educational potential of computer games is immense. To maximize their benefit for the young child in educational settings, however, a number of issues need to be addressed.

Making the context meaningful: on- and off-computer activities

As we have argued, in Chapter 5 for example, one of the key strengths of interactive stories, simulations and adventure games is the way in which they fire the imagination of young children. This will not be achieved nearly so effectively if the program is just left on in a corner of the room, and children play the game at odd moments, unconnected to the rest of their classroom work. Ideally, a computer game should be used as the central stimulus in a work topic or theme. The work the children do with the game should be intimately related to a series of off-computer activities.

Many games lend themselves very naturally to this style of organization, and are, indeed, written with the idea of supporting a learning topic in mind. The various programs based on homes, or fairy tales, or exciting environments such as under the sea, or in a rocket, clearly lend themselves to this kind of extension. Sue Underhay (1989) provided an excellent account of a class project with a slightly older age group based on the program *Flowers of Crystal*. The off-computer work included artwork, scientific and mathematical investigations about crystals, descriptive and informational writing for real purposes, movement work based on the characters in the story, and so on, stimulated by this program.

Organizing collaborative work

A common form of organization when using a computer game in an Early Years classroom or setting is to have the children working in groups. This makes good sense in terms of organization, and, as discussed above, can make a valuable contribution to children's learning.

It is not sufficient, however, simply to put children in random groups and let them get on with it. Composition of groups has been shown in a wide range of research to be crucially important in affecting the amount and quality of verbalization and discussion which occurs (see Dunne and Bennett 1990). Factors which are likely to affect the success of groupwork include size of group, the mix of abilities and gender. All these factors are only significant, however, inasmuch as they affect the quality of talk in the group and the extent to which each individual is genuinely involved in group discussions and decision making. Underwood and Underwood (1990), for example, found that verbalization of plans, negotiation between group members and joint decision making were crucial. Blaye *et al.* (1991) pinpointed the issue of dominance in groups, finding that the most productive groups were ones where one child was not dominating others (which involved predictable gender issues!). In successful groups there was much evidence of turn taking and teamwork with the task divided up into different roles (e.g. controlling the mouse, reading on-screen text, interpreting the map, making notes). There are clear pointers here to the quality of interaction for which we should be looking and the kinds of skills and attitudes we should be attempting to encourage.

ICT *and socio-dramatic play*

Children can learn and be playful and creative with ICT in a variety of ways, but we want to conclude with just two important examples. Symbolic play and socio-dramatic play, in particular, are well established as very important modes of learning for young children (Wood and Attfield 1996). ICT research conducted as a part of the Children's Awareness of Technology (CHAT) project (see http://www.ioe.ac.uk/cdl/CHAT) has shown that the manipulation of symbols and images on the computer screen may actually represent a new form of symbolic play, which the children seem to consider every bit as 'concrete' as the manipulation of any alternative blocks and small-world toys:

> On-screen images were 'grabbed', scolded, fingered and smacked, with dramatic effect, as part of the small-group interaction with the software. In some instances, they took on an off-screen life of their own, as children continued the game the computer had initiated, away from the machine. 'Food' items were one of the favourite symbols for adoption, particularly by the morning 'girls' group':
>
> Tabitha says 'Click'; Alice says 'That won't do anything'; there is group glee when they succeed. All three evolve highly physical and interactive game away from computer: for several minutes they pretend to eat the cheese on the screen, with lots of lip-smacking and appreciative noises and role-play – 'Oh god, it's all gone and I didn't get any!' Annabelle skilfully uses mouse to remove cheese from screen into the limbo of a black border (unconscious control, very skilled). Tabitha says '*Please* can we have another bit?' All three are standing and role-playing: Alice even wipes her fingers on her jumper after 'eating'.
>
> These three, and other girls, frequently 'grabbed' apples and pears from the screen, begged each other to share them, and licked their lips appreciatively after pretending to eat them.
>
> (Brooker and Siraj-Blatchford 2002)

We have argued throughout this book that the research evidence that suggests the value of encouraging young children to communicate playfully and collaborate with their peers and with adults is overwhelming. Any play context that provides a focus for 'joint attention' or 'sustained shared thinking' is significant in this respect. But ICTs have been shown to provide particularly worthwhile opportunities, and we therefore heartily recommend all early childhood practitioners and parents to accept the challenge that this new technology brings.

Glossary of terms

3G (Third Generation) phones: 3G mobile telephones offer greatly improved access to the internet and person-to-person video communication.

ADSL (Asymmetrical digital subscriber line): this converts an ordinary telephone line into a broadband internet connection more than ten times faster than a regular 56Kbps modem (see 'bits per second' below).

Bits: binary digits that can have a value of one or zero (they can be switched 'on' or 'off'). The basis of all the computer's memory, communication and information storage functions.

Bits per second (Bps): the speed at which the computer can communicate (via its modem) with another computer is normally measured in thousands or millions of bits per second (Kbps – Mbps). There are various broadband standards commonly referred to: **T** (or **DS**) **1–4** provide between 1.5 million bits per second (1.5Mbps) and 274 million bits per second (274Mbps). University and industrial users also have access to SONET or **OC 1–48** which may run at between 51Mbps and 2.4 gigabits per second (2.4Gbps).

Broadband: a high-speed internet connection. Often applied to any connections faster than 128Kbps that do not require the user to dial in (see bits per second above).

Browser: applications that let you view pages on the internet (e.g. Internet Explorer, Netscape).

Bytes: a byte is 8 binary bits of data. They are usually referred to in specifying the storage space for thousands of bytes (kilobytes – Kbs), millions of bytes (megabytes – Mbs) or billions of bytes (gigabytes – Gbs). See KiloBytes and GigaBytes.

Central processing unit (CPU): a micro-processor located on the computer's 'motherboard' that controls the main operations of the computer (see processor speed below).

Digital Video Discs (DVDs): store between 4.7 and 17GBs (enough to store a two-hour movie with a soundtrack and interviews etc.).

Domain name: the first step in obtaining a unique web address or domain name is to contact a company who will check availability and register it for you (normally for two years with the right to renew). All of this can be done on the internet in just a few minutes. The price will depend on what you want, so that a top-level domain such as .org or .net may cost as much as £50.00 while a co.uk may be as little as £10.

Firewall: high-speed always-on connections are vulnerable to hacker attacks so software or hardware 'firewalls' are set up to keep them out (see **Hacker** below).

GigaBytes (GBs): billions of bytes. A term normally used to specify the size of hard drives and DVDs.

Hacker: a term that may have been popularly misapplied since the 1960s. Many of the world's best, and most enthusiastic, programmers consider themselves to be hackers, and they apply the alternative term 'cracker' to refer to those (sad) individuals who have nothing better to do than use their skills to gain unauthorized entry to other people's computers and computer networks. (Also see Firewall.)

Hard drive: this is the memory space that the PC uses to store programmes. 6–10 Gigabytes are currently to be expected.

Homepage: the first (main) page of a website which provides the top-level menu. While detailed guidance on how to construct your own website lies beyond the scope of this book, you may well be able to find a parent or other individual who will put something simple for you together for free or for a nominal charge. In this, your first task will be to select and register a domain name (see above). Most internet service providers provide free web space and AOL (for example) also offers simple to use online templates that allow even those with the most basic skills the opportunity to create a web presence in minutes. See: http://www.aol.com/nethelp/publish/aboutpersonalpublisher.html

Hypertext: texts that are linked electronically despite sometimes being served to your browser from computers at different locations.

Hypertext markup language (Html): the programming language used to create pages on a website.

Input devices: these are the devices that are used to input information and/or control the program, e.g. keyboards, the mouse, track balls, touch screens etc.

Integrated services digital network (ISDN): a digital telephone connection providing high-speed data transfer (128Kbs).

Internet: a network of computers liked together. These may be protected from public use as in the case of corporate intranets or they may be freely accessible like the world wide web.

Internet service provider (ISP): these are companies that provide users with modem access to the world wide web. Most ISPs (e.g. America on Line (AOL), BT Internet, Freeserve, and Ntlworld) provide free web space to subscribers as well.

Kilobytes: thousands of bytes. The old 5¼″ floppy discs typically stored 360Kbs, and for a long time the maximum storage of a 3½″ floppy disc was 800Kbs (now typically 1.4MBs).

MegaBytes (MBs): A floppy disc stores 1.4MBs, and that will take the text of an average novel, or about one minute of video. CD-ROMs store 700MBs. See also Bytes, Kilobytes and GigaBytes.

Modem: a device used to connect your computer to the internet. Typically refers to a 56Kbs telephone modem or a broadband cable modem.

Monitor: see Visual Display Unit (VDU) below.

Multimedia: a term used to describe content involving pictures, sound and video.

Operating System (OS): the main software program that runs the computer. The most common operating systems are now Windows (95, 98, 2000, XP), Mac OS (8, 9, 10, X), and UNIX.

Output devices: these are the devices that are used to output information, e.g. the screen, a printer, disc drives, etc.

Pixels: the tiny dots or squares that make up the image on a monitor screen. Picture quality or 'resolution' is measured by the number of pixels, or the dots per inch (dpi) (see Visual Display Unit (VDU) below).

Processor (or clock) speed: modern PCs typically run at 700 megahertz (700MHz) or more, with an Intel Pentium 4 processor running at 2GHz (2000MHz). On the face of it, it might be thought that this means they can carry out 700 million operations, or switch things on and off 700 million times in a second. But there is another specification that must be considered and that is the number of Instructions Per Clock (IPC) cycle. This is important because, while many Apple computers, for example, run at slower clock speeds (e.g. 600MHz), they have relatively high IPCs.

Random Access Memory (RAM): this provides the computer with the temporary storage space it needs to run programs; everything in the RAM is lost when you switch your machine off. 64MBs is now generally considered a minimum specification.

Read Only Memory (ROM): unsurprisingly, this is memory that can only be read.

Scanner: an input device that allows you to copy text, picture or photographs. The crucial specification is the dots per inch (dpi): the higher the dpi the better the resolution (but the bigger the file size).

Server: these are computers that are set up to 'serve' web pages on the internet.

Uniform Resource Locators (URLs): the internet addresses of websites, they typically begin with http://www

Visual Display Unit (VDU): this is another name for the monitor. Cathode ray tubes (CRTs) and liquid crystal displays (LCDs) may be used as screens and CRTs generally give better resolution. Resolution is typically measured by the number of pixels or dots per inch (dpi).

WebCam: A small video camera that usually plugs into the USB socket of your PC. While designed primarily for use on the internet, WebCams provide an inexpensive and versatile means of recording and playing back video for a variety of purposes.

Web space: this is an area of server disc space provided by an internet service provider to allow you to create your own web pages for display on the internet (see home page above).

Wireless Application Protocol (WAP): mobile telephone that allows users to view live news, sport and other internet content and to send and receive email (see also 3G above).

World wide web (www): a 'web' of pages of information and applications that are cross-referenced by hypertext links that allow you to access them with a click of your mouse.

Appendix A
The National Association for the Education of Young Children (NAEYC) Position Statement: Technology and Young Children – Ages 3 through 8

In this position statement, we use the word technology to refer primarily to computer technology, but this can be extended to include related technologies, such as telecommunications and multimedia, which are becoming integrated with computer technology.

Technology plays a significant role in all aspects of American life today, and this role will only increase in the future. The potential benefits of technology for young children's learning and development are well documented (Wright and Shade 1994). As technology becomes easier to use and early childhood software proliferates, young children's use of technology becomes more widespread. Therefore, early childhood educators have a responsibility to critically examine the impact of technology on children and be prepared to use technology to benefit children.

Market researchers tracking software trends have identified that the largest software growth recently has been in new titles and companies serving the early childhood educational market. Of the people who own home computers and have young children, 70 per cent have purchased educational software for their children to use (SPA Consumer Market

Report 1996). While many new titles are good contributions to the field, an even larger number are not (Haugland and Shade 1994).

Early childhood educators must take responsibility to influence events that are transforming the daily lives of children and families. This statement addresses several issues related to technology's use with young children: (1) the essential role of the teacher in evaluating appropriate uses of technology; (2) the potential benefits of appropriate use of technology in early childhood programs; (3) the integration of technology into the typical learning environment; (4) equitable access to technology, including children with special needs; (5) stereotyping and violence in software; (6) the role of teachers and parents as advocates; and (7) the implications of technology for professional development.

NAEYC's *position*

Although now there is considerable research that points to the positive effects of technology on children's learning and development (Clements 1994), the research indicates that, in practice, computers supplement and do not replace highly valued early childhood activities and materials, such as art, blocks, sand, water, books, exploration with writing materials, and dramatic play. Research indicates that computers can be used in developmentally appropriate ways beneficial to children and also can be misused, just as any tool can (Shade and Watson 1990). Developmentally appropriate software offers opportunities for collaborative play, learning, and creation. Educators must use professional judgment in evaluating and using this learning tool appropriately, applying the same criteria they would to any other learning tool or experience. They must also weigh the costs of technology with the costs of other learning materials and program resources to arrive at an appropriate balance for their classrooms.

1. **In evaluating the appropriate use of technology, NAEYC applies principles of developmentally appropriate practice (Bredekamp 1987) and appropriate curriculum and assessment (NAEYC & NAECS/SDE 1992). In short, NAEYC believes that in any given situation, a professional judgment by the teacher is required to determine if a specific use of technology is age appropriate, individually appropriate, and culturally appropriate.**

   The teacher's role is critical in making certain that good decisions are made about which technology to use and in supporting children in their use of technology to ensure that potential benefits are achieved.

Teachers must take time to evaluate and choose software in light of principles of development and learning and must carefully observe children using the software to identify both opportunities and problems and make appropriate adaptations. Choosing appropriate software is similar to choosing appropriate books for the classroom – teachers constantly make judgments about what is age appropriate, individually appropriate, and culturally appropriate. Teachers should look for ways to use computers to support the development and learning that occur in other parts of the classroom and the development and learning that happen with computers in complement with activities off the computer. Good teaching practices must always be the guiding goal when selecting and using new technologies.

2. **Used appropriately, technology can enhance children's cognitive and social abilities.**

Computers are intrinsically compelling for young children. The sounds and graphics gain children's attention. Increasingly, young children observe adults and older children working on computers, and they want to do it, too. Children get interested because they can make things happen with computers. Developmentally appropriate software engages children in creative play, mastery learning, problem solving, and conversation. The children control the pacing and the action. They can repeat a process or activity as often as they like and experiment with variations. They can collaborate in making decisions and share their discoveries and creations (Haugland and Shade 1990).

Well-designed early childhood software grows in dimension with the child, enabling her to find new challenges as she becomes more proficient. Appropriate visual and verbal prompts designed in the software expand play themes and opportunities while leaving the child in control. Vast collections of images, sounds, and information of all kinds are placed at the child's disposal. Software can be made age appropriate even for children as young as three or four.

When used appropriately, technology can support and extend traditional materials in valuable ways. Research points to the positive effects of technology in children's learning and development, both cognitive and social (Clements 1994; Haugland and Shade 1994). In addition to actually developing children's abilities, technology provides an opportunity for assessment. Observing the child at the computer offers teachers a 'window' onto a child's thinking. Just as parents continue to read to children who can read themselves, parents and teachers should both participate with children in computer activities and encourage children to use computers on their own and with peers.

Research demonstrates that when working with a computer children prefer working with one or two partners over working alone (Lipinski et al. 1986; Rhee and Chavnagri 1991; Clements, Nastasi, and Swaminathan 1993). They seek help from one another and seem to prefer help from peers over help from the teacher (King and Alloway 1992; Nastasi and Clements 1993). Children engage in high levels of spoken communication and cooperation at the computer. They initiate interactions more frequently and in different ways than when engaged with traditional activities, such as puzzles or blocks. They engage in more turn taking at the computer and simultaneously show high levels of language and cooperative-play activity.

Technology extends benefits of collaboration beyond the immediate classroom environment for children in the primary grades who can already read and write. With the potential of access to the Internet or other online 'user friendly' networks, young children can collaborate with children in other classrooms, cities, counties, states, and even countries. Through electronic field trips in real time or via diskette, children are able to share different cultural and environmental experiences. Electronic mail and telecommunications opportunities through the Internet facilitate direct communication and promote social interactions previously limited by the physical location of participating learners.

3. **Appropriate technology is integrated into the regular learning environment and used as one of many options to support children's learning.**

Every classroom has its own guiding philosophies, values, schedules, themes, and activities. As part of the teacher's overall classroom plan, computers should be used in ways that support these existing classroom educational directions rather than distort or replace them. Computers should be integrated into early childhood practice physically, functionally, and philosophically. Teachers can accommodate integration in at least five ways:

- Locate computers in the classroom, rather than in a separate computer lab (Davis and Shade 1994).
- Integrate technology into the daily routine of classroom activity. For example, a teacher might introduce musical rhythm with actions, recordings, and a computer used as an electronic rhythm-matching game. The children then would work in small groups with the computer program serving as one of several learning centers.
- Choose software to enrich curriculum content, other classroom activities, or concepts. For example, the program in the computer

learning center might allow children to invent their own rhythms that they could simultaneously hear played back and see displayed graphically. They could edit these rhythms on the computer, hearing and seeing the changes.

- Use technology to integrate curriculum across subject-matter areas. For example, one group of children used the computer to make signs for a restaurant in their dramatic-play area (Apple Computer Inc. 1993). The rhythm program helps children connect mathematical patterns to musical patterns.
- Extend the curriculum, with technology offering new avenues and perspectives. For example, exploring shapes on the computer provides opportunities to stretch, shrink, bend, and combine shapes into new forms. Such activities enrich and extend children's activities with physical manipulatives.

4. **Early childhood educators should promote equitable access to technology for all children and their families. Children with special needs should have increased access when this is helpful.**

   Educators using technology need to be especially sensitive to issues of equity. A decade of research on the educational use of computers in schools reveals that computers maintain and exaggerate inequalities (Sutton 1991). Sutton found gender, race, and social-class inequalities in the educational uses of computers, which Thouvenelle, Borunda, and McDowell summarize below.

- Girls used computers in and out of school less often than did boys.
- African American students had less access to computers than did White students.
- Presence of computers in a school did not ensure access.
- Teachers, while concerned about equity, held attitudes that hindered access – they believed that better behaved students deserved more computer time and that the primary benefit of computers for low-achieving students was mastery of basic skills (i.e., drill-and-practice software).
- Richer schools bought more equipment and more expensive equipment (1994, 153–54).

These findings identify trends that, unchecked, will almost certainly lead to increased inequity in the future. Early childhood educators must find ways to incorporate technology into their classrooms that preserve equity of access and minimize or even reverse the current trends. For example, anecdotal reports indicate that preschool-age boys and girls show equal interest in computers, but as they grow older girls begin to spend less time with computers than do boys. There are a number of ways educators can proactively work to maintain girls' interest in computers and technology: (1) consider girls' interests and interaction styles when selecting and evaluating software for classroom use; (2) model the use of the computer as a learning and productivity tool and invite children, especially girls, to observe and assist them in the work; and (3) promote equity by offering special times for 'girls only' use of computers, which permits girls to explore the computer without having to directly compete with boys (Thouvenelle, Borunda, and McDowell 1994).

Considerations of equity in curriculum content require qualitative judgments. For example, research evidence indicates that children who are economically disadvantaged have less access to computers at home and at-home access is related to attitudes and competence (Martinez and Mead 1988). If schools wish to provide equity to children of low-income families, with respect to their confidence and competence concerning computer learning, these children need to be provided more in-school computer access (Sutton 1991). And that access must be meaningful, moving beyond rote drill-and-practice usage.

Preschool-age children spend time in a variety of diverse settings (e.g., homes, child care centers, family child care), which further complicates the issues of equity and access. Some of these settings have considerable access to technology while others lack the very basics. The more early childhood educators believe in the benefits of appropriate use of technology at the preschool age, the more responsibility we bear in ensuring equity and access to this important learning tool.

Efforts should be made to ensure access to appropriate technology for children with special needs, for whom assistive technologies may be essential for successful inclusion.

For children with special needs, technology has many potential benefits. Technology can be a powerful compensatory tool – it can augment sensory input or reduce distractions; it can provide support for cognitive processing or enhance memory and recall; it can serve as a personal 'on-demand' tutor and as an enabling device that supports independent functioning.

The variety of assistive-technology products ranges from low-tech toys with simple switches to expansive high-tech systems capable of managing complex environments. These technologies empower young children, increasing their independence and supporting their inclusion in classes with their peers. With adapted materials, young children with disabilities no longer have to be excluded from activities. Using appropriately designed and supported computer applications, the ability to learn, move, communicate, and recreate are within the reach of all learners.

Yet, with all these enhanced capabilities, this technology requires thoughtful integration into the early childhood curriculum, or it may fall far short of its promise. Educators must match the technology to each child's unique special needs, learning styles, and individual preferences.

5. **The power of technology to influence children's learning and development requires that attention be paid to eliminating stereotyping of any group and eliminating exposure to violence, especially as a problem-solving strategy.**

Technology can be used to affirm children's diversity.

Early childhood educators must devote extra effort to ensure that the software in classrooms reflects and affirms children's diverse cultures, languages, and ethnic heritages. Like all educational materials, software should reflect the world children live in: it should come in multiple languages, reflect gender equity, contain people of color and of differing ages and abilities, and portray diverse families and experiences (Derman-Sparks and A.B.C. Task Force 1989; Haugland and Shade 1994).

Teachers should actively select software that promotes positive social values. Just like movies and television today, children's software is often violent and much of it explicit and brutally graphic, as in most of the best-selling titles for the popular game machines. But, often, violence is presented in ways that are less obvious. In all of its forms, violence in software threatens young children's development and challenges early childhood educators, who must take active steps to keep it out of their classrooms (see the NAEYC Position Statement on Violence in the Lives of Children 1994).

Some software programs offer children the opportunity to get rid of mistakes by 'blowing up' their creations – complete with sound effects – instead of simply erasing or starting over. As a metaphor for solving problems or getting rid of mistakes, 'blowing up' is problematic. In the context of a computer software experience, it is more troubling than in the context of television or video. Children control the computer software, and, instead of being passive viewers of what appears on the screen, with the computer they become active decisionmakers about what takes place on the screen. Software programs that empower children to freely blow up or destroy without thought of the actual consequences of their actions can further the disconnection between personal responsibility and violent outcomes.

Identifying and eliminating software containing violence is only one of the challenges facing early childhood educators. A related, opposite challenge is discovering software programs that promote positive social actions. For example, software has the potential to offer children opportunities to develop sensitivities to children from other cultures or to children with disabilities. Much could be done to help children develop positive responses to cultural and racial diversity by offering software programs that enable children to explore the richness within their own and different cultures.

6. **Teachers, in collaboration with parents, should advocate for more appropriate technology applications for all children.**

The appropriate and beneficial use of technology with young children is ultimately the responsibility of the early childhood educator, working in collaboration with parents. Parents and teachers together need to make better choices as consumers. As they become educated on the appropriate uses of technology, parents and teachers are more likely to make informed decisions and to make it known to developers of technology when they are unhappy with products. Working together, parents and teachers are a large consumer group wielding greater influence on the development of technology for young children. Following are specific recommendations for early childhood professionals as they advocate for more appropriate technology applications for all children.

- Provide information to parents on the benefits and use of appropriate software.
- Advocate for computer hardware that can be upgraded easily as new technology becomes available.
- Encourage software publishers to make previewing of software easier for parents and educators.
- Advocate for a system of software review by educators.
- Promote the development of software and technology applications that routinely incorporate features that cater to the needs of learners with different abilities.
- Advocate for software that promotes positive representation of gender, cultural and linguistic diversity, and abilities. Software publishers should create a balance of programs that appeal to both boys and girls.
- Encourage software publishers to create programs that support collaboration among learners rather than competition. Fostering cooperative learning enhances the acceptance of the abilities of all learners.

- Encourage software publishers to develop programs that reflect appropriate, nonviolent ways to solve problems and correct mistakes.
- Develop formal and informal information sharing and support for teachers, parents, and appropriate organizations and community-based programs. Encourage free community access to technology through libraries, schools, and so forth.
- Support policies on federal, state, and local levels that encourage funding that supports equity in access to technology for young children and their families.

7. **The appropriate use of technology has many implications for early childhood professional development.**

As early childhood educators become active participants in a technological world, they need in-depth training and ongoing support to be adequately prepared to make decisions about technology and to support its effective use in learning environments for children.

To achieve the potential benefits of technology, both preservice and inservice training must provide early childhood educators with opportunities for basic information and awareness. These efforts must address the rapid proliferation and fast-paced change within the technology arena. Opportunities that emphasize evaluating the software in relation to children's development are essential.

Institutions of higher education and other organizations and groups that provide preservice and inservice education have a responsibility to

- incorporate experiences that permit educators to reflect on the principles of early childhood education and how technology can support and extend these principles;
- give teachers concentrated time to focus on how best to use educational technology and to develop a plan for the use of educational technology in a school or early childhood program;
- provide hands-on training with appropriate software programs to assist teachers in becoming familiar and comfortable with the operation and features of hardware and software; and
- provide on-site and school-based training on effectively integrating technology into the curriculum and assessment process.

At the classroom level, teachers need staff-development experiences (Kearsley and Lynch 1992) that permit them to

- use teaching techniques that fully use the technology;
- encourage parental involvement with technology;

- match technology applications to the learning needs of individual children;
- look for cross-curriculum/cross-cultural applications;
- facilitate cooperative interactions among children; and
- use technology to improve personal efficiency.

The potentials of technology are far-reaching and ever changing. The risk is for adults to become complacent, assuming that their current knowledge or experience is adequate. 'Technology is an area of the curriculum, as well as a tool for learning, in which teachers must demonstrate their own capacity for learning' (Bredekamp and Rosegrant 1994, 61). As teachers try out their new knowledge in the classroom, there should be opportunities to share experiences and insights, problems and challenges with other educators. When teachers become comfortable and confident with the new technology, they can be offered additional challenges and stimulated to reach new levels of competence in using technology.

Early childhood educators should use technology as a tool for communication and collaboration among professionals as well as a tool for teaching children. Technology can be a powerful tool for professional development. Software can provide accessible information and tools for classroom management, planning, and creation of materials. Telecommunications and the Internet can enable teachers to obtain information and new ideas from around the world and to interact with distant experts and peers. Early childhood educators can incorporate principles of cooperative learning as they assist distant peers in acquiring new skills; share curriculum ideas, resources, and promising practices; exchange advice; and collaborate on classroom and professional development projects. Providing training and support for access to services available via online networks and the Internet has the potential of opening the doors to worlds of additional classroom resources. With a responsive online system, mentors can assist novices in becoming more technology literate and more involved in actively using technology for professional benefits. As educators become competent users of technology for personal and professional growth, they can model appropriate use for young children.

References

Apple Computer Inc. 1993. *The adventure begins: Preschool and technology.* Videocassette. (Available from NAEYC.)

Bredekamp, S. (ed.) 1987. *Developmentally appropriate practice in early childhood programs serving children from birth through age 8.* Exp. ed. Washington, DC: NAEYC.

Bredekamp, S. and T. Rosegrant. 1994. Learning and teaching with technology. In *Young children: Active learners in a technological age,* J.L. Wright and D.D. Shade (eds), 53–61. Washington, DC: NAEYC.

Clements, D.H. 1994. The uniqueness of the computer as a learning tool: Insights from research and practice. In *Young children: Active learners in a technological age,* J.L. Wright and D.D. Shade (eds), 31–50. Washington, DC: NAEYC.

Clements, D.H., B.K. Nastasi and S. Swaminathan. 1993. Young children and computers: Crossroads and directions from research. *Young Children* 48 (2): 56–64.

Davis, B.C. and D.D. Shade. 1994. Integrate, don't isolate! – Computers in the early childhood curriculum. *ERIC Digest* (December). No. EDO-PS-94–17.

Derman-Sparks, L. and the A.B.C. Task Force. 1989. *Anti-bias curriculum: Tools for empowering young children.* Washington, DC: NAEYC.

Haugland, S.W. and D.D. Shade. 1990. *Developmental evaluations of software for young children: 1990 edition.* New York: Delmar.

Haugland, S.W. and D.D. Shade. 1994. Software evaluation for young children. In *Young children: Active learners in a technological age,* J.L. Wright and D.D. Shade (eds), 63–76. Washington, DC: NAEYC.

Kearsley, G. and W. Lynch. 1992. Educational leadership in the age of technology: The new skills. *Journal of Research on Computing in Education* 25(1): 50–60.

King, J.A. and N. Alloway. 1992. Preschooler's use of microcomputers and input devices. *Journal of Educational Computing Research* 8: 451–68.

Lipinski, J.A., R.E. Nida, D.D. Shade and J.A. Watson. 1986. The effect of microcomputers on young children: An examination of free-play choices, sex differences, and social interactions. *Journal of Educational Computing Research* 2(2): 147–68.

Martinez, M.E. and N.A. Mead. 1988. Computer competence: The first national assessment. Tech report no. 17-CC-01. Princeton, NJ: National Educational Progress and Educational Testing Service.

NAEYC position statement on violence in the lives of children. 1994. Washington, DC: NAEYC.

NAEYC and NAECS/SDE (National Association of Early Childhood Specialists in State Departments of Education). 1992. Guidelines for appropriate curriculum content and assessment in programs serving children ages 3 through 8. In *Reaching potentials: Appropriate curriculum and assessment for young children,* volume 1, S. Bredekamp and T. Rosegrant (eds), 9–27. Washington, DC: NAEYC.

Nastasi, B.K. and D.H. Clements. 1993. Motivational and social outcomes of cooperative education environments. *Journal of Computing in Childhood Education* 4(1): 15–43.

Rhee, M.C. and N. Chavnagri. 1991. 4 year old children's peer interactions when playing with a computer. *ERIC Digest.* ED 342466.

Shade, D.D. and J.A. Watson. 1990. Computers in early education: Issues put to rest, theoretical links to sound practice, and the potential contribution of microworlds. *Journal of Educational Computing Research* 6(4): 375–92.

SPA consumer market report. 1996. Washington, DC: Software Publishers Association (SPA).

Sutton, R.E. 1991. Equity and computers in the schools: A decade of research. *Review of Educational Research* 61(4): 475–503.

Thouvenelle, S., M. Borunda and C. McDowell. 1994. Replicating inequities: Are we doing it again? In *Young children: Active learners in a technological age,* J.L. Wright and D.D. Shade (eds), 151–66. Washington, DC: NAEYC.

Wright, J.L. and D.D. Shade (eds) 1994. *Young children: Active learners in a technological age.* Washington, DC: NAEYC.

Appendix B
Ergonomics

In Chapter 1 we referred to the serious concerns that have been voiced about the use of desktop computers by young children. The potential hazards of extended use include repetitive strain injury, carpal tunnel damage, effects upon sight, the encouragement of sedentary behaviour and obesity, and the possible risks of radiation exposure from monitors. Our recommendation was that pre-schools followed the DATEC guidance that suggested that 3-year-olds should not be encouraged to sit at a computer for more than 10–20 minutes at a time with a maximum of 40 minutes by the age of 8. Healey (1998) suggests a 15-minute 'eye break' every hour of computer use for children of any age; she also cites the American Academy of Paediatrics who recommend a limit of between 1 and 2 hours per total screen time (TV, video and computer).

Department for Education and Employment (1998) guidance on furniture and equipment in schools suggests that ideally all children's furniture would be individualized. They also recognize that this is impractical and suggest that children aged between 3 and 4 of 'average' height should be sitting at tables 55.5 cms high. We feel that a very good compromise in this may be achieved by talking to the children about the principles of ergonomics, comfort and safety. A good deal can be done to improvise for individual needs using a collection of firm cushions, and, e.g., large construction building blocks. If the children do this for themselves all the better; they will have learnt some important safety principles for the future.

The four basic principles:

1 **The child should be sitting with an upright back and feet flat on the floor.** When feet are left dangling this puts undue pressure on the back of the thigh. It is therefore often suggested that seats that are too small are better than those that are too big. But this will also depend on the height of the table; if a taller chair (or cushions) brings the child up to the level prescribed in 2 below, then it may be better to provide blocks (or even a couple of old telephone books) for the child's feet to rest on.

2 **The child's forearms should be horizontal at 90 degrees relative to the upper arm, with elbows and palms at the same height as the tabletop (keyboard/mouse).** It is also a good idea to encourage children to have their elbows close to the side of their body so that they don't bend their wrists too much.

3 **The monitor should be on a table at least 750 cms deep with the screen positioned for viewing 10–20 degrees below eye level.** This depth, with the top of the monitor aligned roughly with the forehead, allows the children to sit comfortably (about 60 cms) away from the screen without straining their necks.

4 **The child should be using an appropriate size mouse or a trackball.** They result in less strain as they allow the child to use more than one stretched finger.

For more information see:
http://www.eihms.surrey.ac.uk/robens/erg/links.htm
http://www.openerg.com/index.htm

For trackballs and 'mini mice' see:
Granada Learning at: http://www

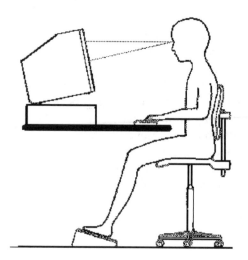

Appendix C
Source of resources referred to in this book

Software by producer

2Simple Software *http://www.2simplesoftware.com/*
2Simple Software
3–4 Sentinel Square
Brent Street
Hendon
London
NW4 2EL
 '2 Go'

4Mation *http://www.4mation.co.uk/*
4Mation Educational Resources
14 Castle Park Road,
Barnstaple
Devon
EX32 8PA
 'Granny's Garden'

Brilliant Computing *http://www.granada-learning.com*
Granada Learning
Quay Street
Manchester
M60 9EA
 'Microworlds 2000'

Brondesbund Living Books *http://www.broderbund.com/*
Mindscape Great Britain
South Block
Forest Gate Business Park
Elm Park Court
Brighton Road
Crawley
West Sussex
RH11 9BP

> *'Just Grandma and Me'*

Dorling Kindersley *http://uk.dk.com*
Dorling Kindersley Limited
The Penguin Group (UK)
80 Strand
London
WC2R ORL

> *'The 3 Little Pigs Interactive Storybook'*

EdMark *http://www.riverdeep.net/edmark/*
Riverdeep Interactive Learning Ltd
Styne House
3rd Floor
Upper Hatch Street
Dublin 2

> *'Millies Math House: Build a Bug'*
> *'Trudy's Time and Place House': The Jelly Bean Hunt*

Fisher Price *http://www.fisher-price.com/uk/*
Fisher Price Ltd.
Mattel House
Vanwall Business Park
Vanwall Road
Maidenhead
Berkshire
SL6 4UB

> *'Pirate Ship'*

Focus MultiMedia *http://www.focusmm.co.uk/*
FM Select Limited,
FREEPOST
MID21599,
Rugeley,
WS15 1BR

> *'Cosmic Family'*

Hasbro *http://www.hasbro.co.uk/*
Hasbro.co.uk Shop
PO Box 57
Newport
NP19 4YE
  'Playschool Store'

Infogrames *http://www.funkidsgames.com/*
Landmark House
Hammersmith Bridge Road
London
W6 9DP
  *'Freddi Fish™ 4: The Case of The Hogfish Rustlers of
  Briny Gulch'*

Logotron *http://www.logo.com/index.php*
124 Cambridge Science Park
Milton Road
Cambridge
CB4 0ZS
  'Thomas the Clown'

Mindscape Entertainment *http://www.learning.co.uk*
Elm Park Court
Tilgate Forest Business Centre
Brighton Rd
Crawley
West Sussex
RH11 9BP
  'Catz', *'Dogz'* and *'Babyz'*

Psygnosis *http://www.psygnosis.com*
Psygnosis
Napier Court
Stephenson Way
Wavertree Technology Park
Liverpool
L13 1EH
  'Lemmings'

Resource *http://www.resourcekt.co.uk/*
Resource Education
51 High Street
Kegworth

Derby
DE74 2DA

> *'Albert's House'*
> *'Music Maker'*
> *'Number 62, Honeypot Lane'*

Sherston *http://www2.sherston.com/*
Sherston Software Limited
Angel House
Sherston
Near Malmesbury
Wiltshire
SN16 0LH

> *'Sherston Naughty Stories'*
> *'Ridiculous Rhymes'*

Tivola Publishing *http://www.tivola.co.uk*
Unit 3c,
21 Coopers Court
Coopers Yard
Newport Pagnell
Milton Keynes
MK16 8JS

> *'Max and the Secret Formula'*
> *'Snow White and the Seven Hansels'*

Topologika Software Ltd *http://www.topologika.co.uk/*
Harbour Village
Penryn
Cornwall
TR10 8LR

> *'MusicBox'*

Hardware by producer

Early Learning Centre *http://www.elc.co.uk/*
ELC Direct
Customer services,
Early Learning Centre,
South Marston Park,
Swindon
SN3 4TJ

> *'Electronic Cash Register'*

Hewlett Packard *http://welcome.hp.com/country/uk/eng/welcome.html*
Cain Road
Amen Corner
Bracknell
Berkshire
RG12 1HN
>'hp scanjet 2300c'

Lego *http://www.lego.com/mybot/*
Customer Services
Capital Point
33 Bath Road
Slough
Berkshire
SL1 3UF
>*'Action Wheelers Remote Control'*
>*'My Bot'*
>*'Lego Mindstorms'*

Sony *http://www.aibo.com/*
The Heights
Brooklands
Weybridge
Surrey
KT13 0XW
>*'Aibo'*
>*'Mavika Digital Camera'*

Swallow Systems *http://www.swallow.co.uk/*
Swallow Systems
134 Cook Lane
High Wycombe
Buckinghamshire
HP13 7EA
>*'Pixie'*
>*'Pip Simulator'*

Valliant Technology *http://www.valiant-technology.com/*
Valiant House
3 Grange Mills
Weir Road
London
SW12 0NE
>*'Roamer'*

Software reviews

http://www.childrenandcomputers.com
http://www.datec.educ.cam.ac.uk
http://www.superkids.com
http://www.TEEM.org
http://www.hitchams.suffolk.sch.uk/foundation/
foundation_ict_reviews.htm

Early childhood sites

Note: We have viewed all of the following sites and found them safe at the time of publication, but we cannot guarantee that they continue to be so. While we have found these sites to be well maintained, all early childhood sites should be checked regularly to ensure that links have not been broken or modified by hackers.

ABC Toon Center: http://www.abctooncenter.com/journal.htm
BBC Games: http://www.bbc.co.uk/cbbc/games/index.shtml
Berit's Best Sites: http://www.beritsbest.com/
Disney Online: www.disney.com
Enchanted Learning Online:
http://www.enchantedlearning.com/categories/pre-school.shtml
Kids @ National Geographic: http://www.nationalgeographic.com/kids/
Kids Domain: http://www.kidsdomain.com/
Kid's Wave: http://www.safesurf.com/kidswave.htm
Knowble Now: http://www.knowble.com
Lulu: http://perso.wanadoo.fr/jeux.lulu/english.htm
Microsoft Kids Website: http://kids.msn.com/kidz/dept.aspx?id=/kidz/content/games/
Peter Rabbit: http://www.peterrabbit.com/
PBS Kids: http://pbskids.org/
Teletubbies: http://www.bbc.co.uk/cbeebies/teletubbies/
The Place For Kids On The Net: http://www.mamamedia.com/
Thomas the Tank Engine: http://www.thomasthetankengine.com/home/homepage.html
Travel in Time with Uder: http://www.uder.co.uk/udermain.html
Up to Ten: http://www.boowakwala.com/
Wcked4kids: http://www.wicked4kids.com/play/index.shtml
Winnie the Pooh: http://www.worldkids.net/pooh/welcome.html
Yahooligans: The Web Guide For Kids: http://www.yahooligans.com/content/games/

Appendix D
Where to find out more

There are two kinds of training normally sought by early years practitioners:

Computer skills training – while this is initially concerned with the basics of how to operate the technology, this should support individuals in developing a basic understanding of how the computer works, and an appreciation of the significance of specifications such as Operating Systems, ROMs, RAMs, processor speeds, screen resolutions etc.

ICT curriculum training – it is this area that has been the central concern of this book. It includes training that is associated with curriculum and classroom organization and pedagogy as well as the evaluation and the development of appropriate ICT activities and applications.

Sources of training

Many pre-schools draw upon the expertise of an individual member of staff, a relative of a member of the staff or a parent to provide computer skills training. Computer suppliers also provide this kind of basic training. Beyond this pre-schools should contact their local 'partnership coordinator' and/or their local education authority. Training may also be available from other nurseries or from local schools, and professional associations such as Early Learning (telephone 020 7539 5400, email: office@early-education.org.uk) are able to provide guidance as well.

See also:

British Educational Communications and Technology Agency (BECTa):
http://www.becta.org.uk
National Grid for Learning (ngfl): http://www.ngfl.gov.uk
National Grid for Learning Scotland; http://www.ngflscotland.gov.uk
Early Education: http://www.early-education.org.uk/

References

Alexandersson, M. and Pramling Samuelsson, I. (1998) *New Ways of Learning. A Project Focusing on How Children Learn Through IT*. Stockholm: Project application to the Swedish National Agency for Higher Education.

Antoniety, A. (1991) *Why Does Mental Visualization Facilitate Problem-solving?* Advances in Psychology Series. New York: North Holland, Elsevier Science Publishers.

Atkinson, S. (ed.) (1992) *Mathematics with Reason*. Sevenoaks: Hodder and Stoughton.

Australian Bureau of Statistics (2001) *Household Use of Information Technology, Australia, November*, Cat. No. 8146.0, Canberra: Commonwealth of Australia. http://www.abs.gov.au/austats/

BECTa (British Educational Communications and Technology Agency) (2001) *Using ICT to enhance home–school links*. London: DfES.

Beeching, R. (2002) *The Insensitive Mouse*. http://www.sierratel.com/robprod/insensitivemouse.htm

Benjamin, J. (2000) 'Net benefits', *Nursery Computing*, October: 4.

Bennett, R. (1997) *Teaching at Key Stage 1: Teaching IT*. Oxford: Nash Pollock.

Blaye, A., Light, P., Joiner, R. and Sheldon, S. (1991) 'Collaboration as a facilitator of planning and problem solving on a computer-based task', *British Journal of Developmental Psychology*, 9: 471–83.

Brooker, E. and Siraj-Blatchford, J. (2002) '"Click on Miaow!": how children of three and four years experience the nursery computer', *Contemporary Issues in Early Childhood*. http://www.triangle.co.uk/ciec/

Bruner, J.S. (1972) 'The nature and uses of immaturity', *American Psychologist*, 27: 1–28.

Bruner, J., Jolly, A. and Sylva, K. (eds) (1976) *Play: Its Role in Development and Evolution*. Harmondsworth: Penguin.

Carter, V. (2001) 'Camelsdale First School email project, Reception, Autumn 2000', *Micros and Primary Education*, Summer.

Cassell, J. (1999) 'Storytelling as a nexus of change in the relationship between gender and technology: a feminist approach to software design', in J. Cassell and H. Jenkins (eds) *From Barbie to Mortal Kombat: Gender and Computer Games*. Cambridge, MA: MIT Press.

CensusAtSchool – is an on-line project providing a database of children's statistics. It is managed by the Royal Statistical Society (RSS) Centre for Statistical Education based at The Nottingham Trent University. Other partners include the Office for National Statistics, the Northern Ireland Statistics and Research Agency and Maths 2000. See: http://www.censusatschool.ntu.ac.uk/default.asp

CensusAtSchool (2000) *CensusAtSchool* Results, http://www.censusatschool.ntu.ac.uk/results.asp

Clements, D.H. and Gullo, D.F. (1984) 'Effects of computer programming on young children's cognition', *Journal of Educational Psychology*, 76: 1051–8.

Cox, Margaret (1997) *The Effects of Information Technology on Students' Motivation*, Final report. King's College London: National Council for Educational Technology (now BECTa).

Craft, A. (2000) *Creativity across the Primary Curriculum*. London: Routledge.

Crook, C. (1987) 'Computers in the classroom: defining a social context', in J. Rutkowska and C. Crook (eds) *Computers, Cognition and Development*. Chichester: Wiley.

Crook, C. (1994) *Computers and the Collaborative Experience of Learning*. London: Routledge.

Davis, B. (1989) *Frogs and Snails and Feminist Tails*. St Leonards, NSW, Australia: Allen and Unwin.

Deacon, T. (1997) *The Symbolic Species: The Co-evolution of Language and the Human Brain*. London: Penguin.

De Boo, M. (ed.) (1999) *Science 3–6: Laying the Foundations in the Early Years*. Hatfield: Association for Science Education (ASE).

De Loache, J.S. and Brown, A. (1987) 'The early emergence of planning skills in children', in J. Bruner and H. Haste (eds) *Making Sense: The Child's Construction of the World*. London: Methuen.

DfEE (Department for Education and Employment) (1998) *Furniture and Equipment in Schools: A Purchasing Guide*. London: The Stationery Office.

DfES (Department for Education and Skills) (2001) Information and Communications Technology in Schools in England: 2001, http://www.dfes.gov.uk/statistics/DB/SFR/s0284/sfr 36–2001.doc

DfES (Department for Education and Skills) (2002) *Transforming the Way We Learn: A Vision for the Future of ICT in Schools*. London: DfES/National Grid for Learning.

Doise, W. and Mugny, G. (1984) *The Social Development of the Intellect*. Oxford: Pergamon Press.

Dunne, E. and Bennett, N. (1990) *Talking and Learning in Groups*. London: Macmillan.

Edwards, C. and Hiler, C. (1993) *A Teacher's Guide to the Exhibit: The Hundred Languages of Children*. Lexington, KY: College of Human Environmental Sciences, University of Kentucky.

Edwards, C. and Springate, K. (1995) 'The lion comes out of the stone: helping young children achieve their creative potential', *Dimensions of Early Childhood*, 23 (4): 24–9.

Ellul, J. (1980) *The Technological System* (translated by J. Neugroschel). New York, NY: Continuum.

Epstein, D. (1995) ' "Girls don't do Bricks": gender and sexuality in the primary classroom', in Siraj-Blatchford, J. and Siraj-Blatchford, I. (eds) *Educating the Whole Child: Cross Curricular Skills, Themes and Dimensions*. Milton Keynes: Open University Press.

Epstein, J. (1996) 'Perspective and previews on research and policy for school, family and community partnerships', in A. Booth and J. Dunn (eds) *Family–School Links: How Do They Affect Educational Outcomes?* Mahwah, NJ: Lawrence Erlbaum.

Escobedo, T. and Evans, S. (1997) A comparison of child-tested early childhood education software with professional ratings: Paper presented at the American Education Research Association (AERA) Annual Conference, Chicago, March.

Facer, K., Furlong, J., Sutherland, R. and Furlong, R. (2000) 'Home is where the hardware is: young people, the domestic environment and "access" to new technologies', in I. Hutchby and J. Moran-Ellis (eds) *Children, Technology and Culture*. London: Falmer.

Fanning, J. (2001) *Expanding the Definition of Technological Literacy in Schools*. http://www.mcrel.org/topics/noteworthypages/noteworthy/jimf.asp

Fields, J. (1991) 'Information technology in the early years classroom: a case study', *Early Child Development and Care*, 69: 53–62.

Fine, C. and Thornbury, M.L. (2000) 'Children in control', in M. Monteith (ed.) *IT for Learning Enhancement*, Revised Edition. Exeter: Intellect Books.

Fisher, R. (1987) *Problem-solving in Primary Schools*. Oxford: Basil Blackwell.

Fletcher-Flinn, C.M. and Suddendorf, T. (1996) 'Computer attitudes, gender and exploratory behaviour: a developmental study', *Journal of Educational Computing Research*, 15(2): 97–112.

Flynn, J.R. (1994) 'IQ gains over time', in R.J. Sternberg (ed.) *Encyclopaedia of Human Intelligence*, pp. 617–23. New York, NY: Macmillan.

Forman, E. (1989) 'The role of peer interaction in the social construction of mathematical knowledge', *International Journal of Educational Research*, 13: 55–69.

Francis, H. (1987) 'Cognitive implications of learning to read', *Interchange*, 18: 97–108.

Furlong, J., Furlong, R., Facer, K. and Sutherland, R. (2000) 'The National Grid for Learning: a curriculum without walls?', *Cambridge Journal of Education*, 30(1).

Giacquinta, B.J., Baucer, A.J. and Levin, J. (1993) *Beyond Technology's Promise*. Cambridge: Cambridge University Press.

Gill, T. (ed.) (1996) *Electronic Children: How Children are Responding to the Information Revolution*. London: National Children's Bureau.

Gourdji, A. (1998) *A Question of Gender: The Queens Amiga Users Group* (QAUG), February, http://www.escape.com/~joeg/gender.html

Guha, M. (1987) 'Play in school', in G.M. Blenkin and A.V. Kelly (eds) *Early Childhood Education: A Developmental Curriculum*. London: Paul Chapman.

Hall, N. (1989) *Writing with Reason*. Sevenoaks: Hodder and Stoughton.

Healey, J. (1998) *Failure to Connect*. New York, NY: Simon and Schuster.

Healy, J. (2001) 'Computers rot our children's brains', *Observer*, 16 April.

Hoyles, C. (1985) 'What is the point of group discussion in mathematics?', *Studies in Mathematics*, 16: 205–24.

Hundeide, K. (1991) *Helping Disadvantaged Children: Psycho-Social Intervention and Aid to Disadvantaged Children in Third World Countries*. London: Jessica Kingsley.

Hutchby, I. and Moran-Ellis, J. (eds) (2001) *Children, Technology and Culture: The Impacts of Technologies in Children's Everyday Lives*. London: Routledge Falmer.

Intercultural Development Research Association (IDRA) (2001) *Newsletters*. Available at http://www.idra.org

Jackson, A., Fletcher, B. and Messer, D. (1986) A survey of microcomputer use and provision in primary schools, *Journal of Computer Assisted Learning*, 2: 45–55.

Jones, M. and Min Liu (1997) 'Introducing interactive multimedia to young children: a case study of how two year olds interact with the technology', *Journal of Computing in Childhood Education*, 8(4): 313–43.

Kaput, J. (1996) 'Technology, curriculum and representation: rethinking the foundations and the future', in W. Doerfler *et al.* (eds) *Schriftenreihe Didaktik der Mathematik, Trends und Perspektiven*. Vienna: Hoelder-Pichler-Tempsky.

Laurel, B. (ed.) (1990) *The Art of Human-Computer Interface Design*. Reading, MA: Addison-Wesley.

Lawler, R.W. (1985) *Computer Experience and Cognitive Development*. Chichester: Ellis Harwood.

Levin, C. (2001) How do very young children relate to new technologies? Paper presented at 6th ITTE Research Seminar, University of Cambridge.

Light, P. and Butterworth, G. (eds) (1992) *Context and Cognition: Ways of Learning and Knowing*. Hemel Hempstead: Harvester Wheatsheaf.

Linderoth, J. (2000) *Graphical Awareness: An Exemplar of Good Practice from the Developmentally Appropriate Technology in Early Childhood (DATEC) Project*. http://www.ioe.ac.uk/cdl/datec/datecfrm1.htm

Littler, M. (1999) 'Touching technology', *Resource Manager Today*, May: 9–10.

Littleton, K., Light, P., Joiner, R., Messer, D. and Barnes, P. (1998) 'Gender, task scenarios and children's computer-based problem solving', *Educational Psychology*, 18: 327–40.

Loveless (1995) *The Role of IT: Practical Issues for the Primary Teacher*. London: Cassell.

McFarlane *et al.* (2000) *Teachers Evaluating Educational Multimedia*. London: DfES.

Melhuish, E., Sylva, K., Sammons, P., Siraj-Blatchford, I. and Taggart, B (2001) *The Effective Provision of Pre-School Education (EPPE) Project Technical Paper 7: Social/Behavioural and Cognitive Development at 3–4 Years in Relation to Family Background*. Report to the DfES. London: University of London Institute of Education.

Miller, G.A., Galanter, E. and Pribram, K.H. (1960) *Plans and the Structure of Behaviour*. New York, NY: Holt, Rinehart and Winston.

Mitchell, P. (1997) *Introduction to Theory of Mind*. London: Arnold.

Moyles, J.R. (1989) *Just Playing? The Role and Status of Play in Early Childhood Education*. Milton Keynes: Open University Press.

Mumtaz, S. (2001) 'Children's enjoyment and perception of computer use in the home and the school', *Computers and Education*, 36: 347–62.

Next Generation Forum (1999) *Next Generation Annual Report*. http://www.nextgenerationforum.org; http://www.mm.dk/forum/forum_projekter_nextgen.htm

Offir, B. (1993) 'C.A.I. as a factor in changing the self image of pre-school children', in Y. Katz (ed), *Computers in Education: Pedagogical and Psychological Implications*, pp. 68–74. Unesco.

Olson, D.R., Torrance, N. and Hildyard, A. (eds) (1985) *Literacy Language and Learning: The Nature and Consequences of Reading and Writing*. Cambridge: Cambridge University Press.

Papert, S. (1981) *Mindstorms: Children, Computers and Powerful Ideas*. New York, NY: Basic Books.

Papert, S. (1998) From an interview in New York, cited in P. Arden, S. Papert, in P. Stanbrook (ed), *The Whistleblowers*. Nottingham, Education Now Books.

Papert, S. (2001) Cited in the Frontline Editorial, *TechKnowlogia*, September/October. http://www.TechKnwLogia.org

Podmore, V. (1991), '4-year-olds, 6-year-olds and microcomputers. A study of perceptions and social behaviour', *Journal of Applied Developmental Psychology*, 12(1): 87–101.

Qualifications and Curriculum Agency (1999) *The National Curriculum: Handbook for Primary Teachers in England*, Key Stages 1 and 2. London: HMSO.

QCA/DfEE (Qualifications and Curriculum Authority/Department for Education and Employment) (2000) *Curriculum Guidance for the Foundation Stage: Stepping Stones*. London: QCA/DfEE.

Robinson, E. (1983) 'Metacognitive development', in S. Meadows (ed.) *Developing Thinking: Approaches to Children's Cognitive Development*. London: Methuen.

Sanger, J., Willson, J., Davies, B. and Whittaker, R. (1997) *Young Children, Videos and Computer Games: Issues for Teachers and Parents*. London: Falmer Press.

SCAA (Schools Curriculum and Assessment Authority) (1995) *Key Stages 1 and 2 Information Technology: The New Requirements*. London: SCAA.

Schaffer, R. (1977) *Mothering*. London: Fontana.

Schweinhart, L. and Weikart, D. (1997) 'The High/Scope pre-school curriculum comparison through age 23', *Early Childhood Research Quarterly*, 12, pp. 117–43.

Sefton-Green, J. (ed.) (1999) *Young People, Creativity and New Technologies*. London: Routledge.

Sherman, W.R. and Craig, A.B. (1995) 'Literacy in virtual reality: a new medium', *Computer Graphics*, 29(4) November: 37–41.

Shoffner, L.B. (1990) 'The effects of home environment on achievement and attitudes towards computer literacy', *Educational Research Quarterly*, 14: 6–14.

Siraj-Blatchford, I., Sylva, K., Muttock, S. and Gilden, R. (2001) *Effective Pedagogy in the Early Years: A Report to the DfEs*. London: University of London Institute of Education.

Siraj-Blatchford, I. and Siraj-Blatchford, J. (2003) *More than Computers: Information and Communication Technology in the Early Years*. The British Association for Early Childhood Education.

Siraj-Blatchford, J. (2003) *Developing New Technologies for Young Children*. Stoke on Trent: Trentham Books.

Siraj-Blatchford, J. and MacLeod-Brudenell, I. (2000) *Supporting Science Design and Technology in the Early Years*. Buckingham: Open University Press.

Siraj-Blatchford, J. and Siraj-Blatchford, I. (2002a) *IBM KidSmart Early Learning Programme: UK Evaluation Report – Phase 1 (2000–2001)*, IBM White Paper. London: IBM.

Siraj-Blatchford, J. and Siraj-Blatchford, I. (2002b) 'Developmentally appropriate technology in early childhood: "video conferencing" ', *Contemporary Issues in early Childhood*, 3(2): 216–25.

Siraj-Blatchford, J. and Siraj-Blatchford, I. (2003) *A Curriculum Development Guide to ICT in Early Childhood Education*, published in collaboration with *Early Education*. Stoke on Trent: Trentham Books.

Straker, A. (1993) *Children Using Computers*. Oxford: Blackwell.

Suddendorf, T. and Fletcher-Flinn, C. (1997) 'Theory of mind and the origins of divergent thinking', *Journal of Creative Behavior*, 31: 169–79.

Swade, D. (2000) *The Cogwheel Brain: Charles Babbage and the quest to build the first computer*. London: Little Brown.

Sylva, K., Bruner, J. and Genova, P. (1976) 'The role of play in the problem-solving of children 3–5 years old', in J.S. Bruner, A. Jolly and K. Sylva (eds) *Play: Its Role in Development and Evolution*. Harmondsworth: Penguin.

Sylva, K. and Nabuco, M. (1996) 'Research on quality in the curriculum', *International Journal of Early Childhood*, 28(2): 1–6.

Sylva, K. and Wiltshire, J. (1993) 'The impact of early learning on children's later development: a review prepared for the RSA inquiry "Start Right" ', *European Early Childhood Education Research Journal*, 1: 17–40.

Taylor Nelson Sofres (2002) 'Young people and ICT', reported in DfES, *Transforming the Way We Learn: A Vision for the Future of ICT in Schools*. London: DFES/National Grid for Learning.

Thouvenelle, S., Borunda, M. and McDowell, C. (1994) Replicating inequities: are we doing it again? in J. Wright and D. Shade (eds) *Young Children: Active Learners in a Technological Age*. Washington, DC: NAEYC.

Turkle, S. (1998) 'Cyborg babies and cy-dough-plasm: ideas about self and life in the culture of simulation', in R. Davis-Floyd and J. Dumit (eds) *Cyborg Babies, Techno-Sex to Techno-Tots*. New York, NY: Routledge.

Underhay, S. (1989) 'Project work: adventure Games', in R. Crompton (ed.) *Computers and the Primary Curriculum 3–13*. Lewes: Falmer Press.

Underwood, J. and Underwood, G. (1990) *Computers and Learning: Helping Children Acquire Thinking Skills*. Oxford: Basil Blackwell.

US Department of Commerce (2000) *Falling through the Net: Toward Digital Inclusion*. The National Telecommunications and Information Administration (NTIA). http://www.ntia.doc.gove/ntiahome/fttn00/contents00.html

Wajcman, J. (1991) *Feminism Confronts Technology*. Cambridge: Polity Press.

Walkerdine, V. (1981) 'Sex, power and pedagogy', *Screen Education*, 38: 14–24.

Watson, J. and Ramey, C. (1972) 'Reactions to response-contingent stimulation in early infancy', *Merrill-Palmer Quarterly*, 18: 219–27.

WhichOnline (2002a) *Annual Internet Survey: 2002*. http://www.which.net/surveys/survey2002.pdf

WhichOnline (2002b) *Pre-school Software*. http://sub.which.net/ict/reports/oct2001pt22t24/printrerort.html

Whitebread, D. (1997) 'Developing children's problem-solving: the educational uses of adventure games', in A. McFarlane (ed.) *Information Technology and Authentic Learning*. London: Routledge.

Wills, C. (1994) *The Runaway Brain: The Evolution of Human Uniqueness*. London: HarperCollins.

Wood, D. (1998) *How Children Think and Learn*, 2nd edn. Oxford: Basil Blackwell.

Wood, E. and Attfield, J. (1996) *Play, Learning and the Early Childhood Curriculum*. London: Paul Chapman.

Index